Shadsworth Neighbourhood Centre.

Teenscape

Teenscape

A personal safety programme for teenagers

Second edition

Michele Elliott

Published in 1995
Health Education Authority
Hamilton House
Mabledon Place
London WC1H 9TX

© Michele Elliott

ISBN 0 7521 0279 6

A CIP catalogue record for this book is available from the British
Library.

Michele Elliott has asserted her right under the Copyright, Designs
and Patents Act, 1988, to be identified as Author of this Work.

The views expressed in this book are those of the author and not
necessarily those of the Health Education Authority.

Typeset by DP Photosetting, Aylesbury, Bucks
Printed by Scotprint, Musselburgh

Contents

Acknowledgements

Teenscape and the Revised Teenscape is the result of years of work and help from hundreds of people. It is impossible to thank everyone and if you don't find yourself listed below, please consider yourself appreciated and my memory faulty:

Miggie Hillson, Jane Hood and Kate Hill, The Grey Coat Hospital School, London

Lyle Riggs, TASIS School, Surrey

Valerie Besag, Educational Psychologist, Gateshead

Dan Olweus, Professor of Psychology, University of Bergen, Norway

John Ruddick, County Welfare Officer, East Sussex

Derek Driver, Metropolitan Police

Dave Williams, Kent Police

Gill Robinson, Senior Advisory Teacher, Birmingham

Linda Frost, Headteacher, Montem School

Nicholas Hargreaves, who contributed the excellent 'Bully diary'

John Hadjipateras, who has supported Kidscape throughout

Hodder/Headline Publishers who allowed me to reproduce the Teen questionnaires from *Keeping safe: a practical guide to talking with children*, 1994 edition

Charles and James Elliott, my teenage children who are my best critics

Edward Elliott, my patient and much 'put-upon' husband

Daphne Joiner, who not only works in the office, but keeps the home fires burning

A final word of thanks to the Kidscape Staff, who support all the writing and keep me going with their humour:

Jane Kilpatrick

Linda Llewellyn

Angela Glasser

Sue Woods

Daphne Joiner

Lisa Flowers

Unit 1   User's Guide

Introduction

Teenscape is a comprehensive approach to teaching 'good sense defence'. This concept teaches young people positive and practical ways for dealing with potentially dangerous situations. It incorporates all the successful elements of several pilot studies and makes it possible for parents, teachers and other concerned adults to teach young people in a low-key, non-frightening and practical way to get help and to try to keep themselves out of danger, if possible.

Teenscape is based on the premise that:

- All teenagers and children have the right as individuals to knowledge that will help them to be safe, to be independent and to be able to express their own feelings and concerns.
- All adults have the responsibility to keep teenagers and children safe, to listen to their feelings and concerns and take them seriously.

Teenscape consists of four units. Each unit deals with a different aspect of the programme:

Unit 1   User's guide
Unit 2   Planning the programme
Unit 3   Meeting for parents
Unit 4   Teenscape lessons

This Unit deals with

- an overview of Teenscape
- information about Kidscape
- information about bullying and child abuse
- Kidscape leaflet – 'Anti-bullying policy for schools'
- 'fact sheets':
  — criminal offences
  — implementation schedule for schools
  — references.

Unit 1 is divided into three chapters:

Chapter 1 – Using the manual
Explains the way the manual is set up and gives an overview of what is in the Teenscape programme.

Chapter 2 – Kidscape

Gives the background about Kidscape and some of the pilot studies that were done in setting up the programmes.

Chapter 3 – Background Information

Gives information about bullying and child abuse, which can be referred to when running the parents' meeting.

Chapter 1   Using the Manual

What is it?

This manual provides a comprehensive approach to teaching 'good sense defence' to teenagers.

Teenscape was originally the result of an extensive two year pilot project run by Kidscape which involved 4000 children and their parents and teachers in schools in the UK. The pilot project was so successful and the demand so great that three Kidscape programmes were subsequently developed for different age groups (under fives, primary and teens) that could easily be used by anyone working with children. Knowing the time constraints and the amount of work facing teachers and others, we have ensured that Teenscape can be taught without masses of extra time. Basically, if you can work effectively with young people, you can teach them good sense defence.

The Kidscape programmes are being used by over 2 million children in the UK, and the numbers are growing. Although Teenscape and the other programmes are curriculum based, they are being used by health visitors, school nurses, education welfare officers, educational psychologists, police officers, residential care workers, youth leaders and social workers, as well as by teachers. In short, this manual is for anyone in a position to teach good sense defence to teenagers.

What is in it?

Manual

The manual consists of four units.

Unit 1 tells you what is in the manual and how to use it. It also gives background information about bullying, child abuse and Kidscape, as well as a further resources guide.

Unit 2 gives information about which agencies might be involved and how to develop Teenscape.

Unit 3 provides a script for the parents' meeting which explains Teenscape to parents.

Unit 4 is the heart of the manual and provides lessons to teach young people good sense defence.

Leaflets

Included in Units 1 and 3 are examples of three leaflets that can be given to parents and staff. The leaflet in Unit 1 is a Kidscape whole-school anti-bullying policy, including signs which might indicate that a child is being bullied. The first leaflet in Unit 3 gives basic information about child abuse; the second explains the Teenscape Child Protection Programme. You may wish to prepare similar leaflets and distribute them to parents or to staff or to other professionals who are involved with your school or institution.

How to use the manual

The Teenscape manual takes you through all the steps for involving adults and teaching young people 'good sense defence'. It is easy to use. The lessons for teenagers and the meeting for parents are both scripted, in case you do not have the time to set up your own plans. Of course, the scripts are often used as a basis for working out a suitable lesson or meeting which might be more appropriate for your school or institution. The manual is a guide, and is not meant to be prescriptive.

We suggest reading through the entire manual before beginning the lessons with students. If this is not possible, leaf through the manual and watch out for the most important information. This might be instructions about using the manual or points to be emphasised in meetings with staff or with parents. Unit 4, which contains the lessons, is the heart of the manual.

Chapter 2   Kidscape

What is Kidscape?

Kidscape is a registered charity founded in 1984 by Michele Elliott. The aims of Kidscape are to ensure that children have access to personal safety education and that the adults who are in contact with children have enough information to help keep children safe. **The underlying philosophy of Kidscape is that all young people and children have the right to be safe and that adults have the responsibility to ensure that safety.**

Michele Elliott is a teacher and educational psychologist, who began working with children and families in 1968. She has chaired Home Office and World Health Organization committees and is the author of numerous books and articles about the subject of child safety and the prevention of child abuse. Although American born, she has lived and worked in the UK since 1971 and is a dual citizen of both the UK and the USA. She is on the Advisory Boards of ChildLine and the National Society for the Prevention of Cruelty to Children (NSPCC), and is a Winston Churchill Fellow. She is married and has two teenage sons.

Pilot projects

The Kidscape Child Protection Programmes are based on three pilot projects. The first project (1984–1986) involved a two-year study with 4000 children and their parents and teachers. It was set up in 1984 and was the first nationwide prevention programme for children dealing with the issue of personal safety. Although 'stranger danger' was widely taught to children by police schools liaison officers, it was found that the main threat to children's safety was from people known to them – bullies, friends, even family members.

After gathering information on programmes from several countries, visiting schools and taking part in training courses with the Child Assault Prevention Project in Ohio, USA, the first Kidscape pilot was undertaken. Consultation with the NSPCC, the Department of Health, the police, social service departments, psychiatrists, psychologists, teachers, health workers and others working with children helped to establish the best way to implement the pilot project.

Although the initial ideas were based upon the Child Assault Prevention Project from the USA, it became clear that the material and methods from other countries were not totally suitable for schools in the UK. The Kidscape programme needed to be curriculum based, taught by people the children knew and it had to have a wide basis of child personal. Many of the US programmes concentrated only on abuse, but we felt that the Kidscape programme needed to incorporate the issues of bullying, stranger danger, child abuse and other potential problems such as getting lost, telling an adult when something was not right, and strategies the children could practise in order to get away and get help whenever possible.

The initial pilot project involved parents, teachers, police, education welfare officers, school nurses and children in meetings and lessons. The first programme was completed in November 1984 at the TASIS school in Surrey. Feedback from everyone concerned was excellent. The programme was described by those who took part as informative, fun, practical, non-threatening, low-key and interesting. Subsequently, 4000 children took part in the full pilot project which included a comparison between three pilot schools and three control schools. Following is a brief outline of the original pilot project and information about the reactions of children, parents and staff in schools.

Parents

Parents of all the children were invited to meetings.

- Parent meetings were well attended – approximately 80% of the children involved were represented by at least one parent or guardian. We think the attendance was so high because the subject of children's personal safety was new in 1984–6 and parents were anxious to discover what their children were being taught. In subsequent pilots, parental interest was not as high.
- Parents were given the option of withdrawing their children from the programme; only six chose to do this.
- Approximately 20% of parents said that they or someone in their family had been sexually abused.

Schools and organisations

The pilot programme was undertaken in:

- 14 schools
- 1 play association
- 15 smaller groups such as scout troops, church and youth clubs

Staff

In all, 200 teachers, school nurses, education welfare officers, police and youth leaders were involved in teaching the lessons.

- Only one teacher chose not to be involved, for personal reasons.
- A total of 65 members of staff took part in the roleplays with children.
- Teachers remained with their classes during the workshops.

Teenagers and children

A total of 4000 teenagers and children were taught the Kidscape Protection Programmes. During the programmes, teenagers and children were encouraged to tell of any experiences which had upset them or made them feel unhappy or worried:

- 2720 teenagers and children (68%) said they had been bullied during the previous year.
- 480 teenagers and children (12%) said that they had been severely bullied and that it had affected their lives to the extent that they did not want to go to school, had attempted suicide, had run away or played truant, had had nightmares and illnesses; their family life had also been badly affected.
- 3400 teenagers and children (85%) recounted having been lost at some point in their lives.
- 280 teenagers and children (7%) told of physical abuse.
- 440 teenagers and children (11%) told of sexually abusive experiences. Of these:
  — 229 (52%) reported obscene telephone calls and flashers
  — 176 (40%) reported that someone known to them had touched or kissed them in an inappropriate way. Most of these incidents had occurred in the past, though 65 cases were referred to social services or the police
  — 35 (8%) reported sexually abusive experiences involving incest, attempted rape or buggery, rape, oral sex or a combination of these offences.

In all cases, teenagers and children were given support by teachers, social workers, parents, police and whichever agencies were appropriate.

We have no way of knowing if the experiences of these 4000 children and teenagers are representative of the population as a whole or if they were unique to our sample. We did, however, conduct a control study to determine if the Kidscape Protection Programmes were successful in teaching children ways to stay safe and in encouraging children to tell about abusive experiences.

Control study

The study was conducted over a three-month period. The staff of the pilot schools were questioned before the programme was introduced to the children about the number of disclosures of abusive experiences they had had from teenagers and children during the past year. The staff of the control schools were also questioned. The control schools did not have the programme introduced until three months later than the pilot schools and the children in these schools had no input about personal safety from the staff during this time. When we compared the results, we found:

	Pilot schools (3)	Control schools (3)
Number of children	795	732
Number of disclosures before the programme	0	0
Number of disclosures immediately after the programme or within three months	89	0
Reports of children keeping safe from bullies, strangers before programme	0	0
Reports of children keeping safe from bullies, strangers immediately after the programme or within three months	6	0
Known false allegations	0	0

We also asked the staff of the pilot schools to observe if the teenagers and children were upset in any way by the programme and sent out questionnaires to all the parents as well. They reported that, within the three months after the study, no children had come to their notice who had been upset by the programme. We also asked the teenagers and children themselves to fill out questionnaires or helped the younger ones to do so.

Teenagers and childrens' questionnaire

A questionnaires was distributed to children and teenagers to determine their reactions. They were asked:

1. Did you like the lessons?
2. Which parts did you like best
3. Did anything in the lessons frighten you?
4. What do you remember best from the lessons?
5. If you had a problem, whom could you go to for help?

    The answers indicated that:

1. 96% of the children and teenagers liked the lessons.

2. The younger children enjoyed the roleplays and stories best, particularly the bully roleplays. The teenagers enjoyed the group discussions, questionnaires and 'self-defence' lessons best.

3. All of them said the lessons were not frightening.

4. Teenagers remembered the lessons about bullying and safety when out, as well as lessons about saying 'no'. Children remembered the lessons about strangers and bullying.

5. The children and teenagers listed many different people they could tell, especially friends, grans, mums, and school nurses and pastoral teachers.

Parents' questionnaire

The parents were given the following questionnaire to determine their and their children's and teenagers' reactions to the lessons. The responses are given in square brackets.

Following the Kidscape programmes, we are interested in how you feel it has or has not affected your child and/or teenager. Would you please take five minutes to answer the following questions:

1. Do you feel that your child's response to being taught 'Good Sense Defence' was
positive [98%] negative [0%] made no difference [02%]

2. Do you feel it has affected your child's response to affection in any way? With members of the family, is your child
more affectionate [05%] less affectionate [0%] the same [95%]

3. Do you feel that Kidscape has affected your relationship with your child? Are you
more affectionate [12%] less affectionate [0%] the same [88%]

4. Since learning 'Good sense defence', do you feel that your child is
more confident [76%] less confident [0%] the same [24%]

5. How do you feel about talking with your child about safety issues, since taking part in the parent's meeting:
more confident [97%] less confident [0%] the same [03%]

6. Do you think children and teenagers should be taught the Kidscape protection programmes?
yes [99%] no [0%] undecided [1%]

Since being involved in the Kidscape programmes, has your child and/or teenager:

7. Told you about any inappropriate behaviour towards the child or any other child?
   Yes [5%] No [95%]
   If yes, please explain: [several parents were told by their children of abuse]

8. Used any of the techniques taught in the lessons (i.e. bullies, strangers, being lost, making telephone calls, known adult)
   yes [12%] no [88%]
   If yes, please explain: [12% of the parents said their children had *told* them about using Kidscape methods to keep safe]

9. Is there anything you would like to say about the Kidscape programme or any suggestions you would like to make?
   [Parents suggested that children have lessons every term, that Kidscape was good because it did not frighten their children and the idea of using roleplays was excellent. Most parents used this space to say thank you for giving their children and/or teenagers the programme.]

Upsetting children and teenagers

Throughout the pilot study, we were concerned that:

- none of children or teenagers would be upset by the contents of the lessons;
- teenagers and children would be able to learn the safety messages easily and would remember them;
- teenagers and children would be able to keep safe should a real danger confront them.

From the data we collected from teachers, parents and the children themselves, we know we succeeded in not upsetting the children or teenagers.

Chapter 3   Background Information

Bullying

Since Kidscape conducted the first nationwide survey of bullying in 1984 to 1986, there have been numerous other surveys in the UK.

Kidscape found that, of the 4000 teenagers and children surveyed:

- 68% reported being bullied within the previous year, but it must be noted that this included sibling bullying and 'falling out' with friends, as well as single incidents which were not considered too serious. Nevertheless, the children had experienced bullying behaviour;
- 38% of the children had been bullied either more than once or they experienced a particularly terrifying incident;
- 8% of the boys and 4% of the girls reported severe bullying which had affected their everyday lives to the extent that they played truant from school, had psychosomatic illness, were school phobic or had attempted suicide. This type of bullying was ongoing, consistent and soul destroying (Elliott 1991);
- 5% admitted to being bullies themselves

The acknowledged expert in bullying behaviour, Professor Dan Olweus of Norway, conducted a nationwide survey of bullying. On the basis of the survey, he estimated that 15% of the students in Norwegian schools were involved in bully/victim problems. He also concluded that being a bully or a victim is something that can last for several years and that special efforts need to be made to help children out of these roles. Olweus's research indicates that strong anti-bullying measures, including increased supervision and class rules, can help alleviate the problem. He also noted that sanctions were necessary in order to change the behaviour of aggressive students: 'it is usually not enough for the teacher (or other adults) to be benevolently understanding and to dispense a good deal of praise. Research and experience show that one must also make use of sanctions – some form of negative consequences – for undesirable behaviour' (Olweus 1993).

Stephenson and Smith gathered information on 1000 children in 26 schools. They found that approximately 25% of the children were involved in bullying, either as victims or as bullies, and that bullying was a persistent problem. In about 80% of the cases, the bullying had gone on for a year or longer. Of particular interest were the findings that bullying was discouraged by:

- a school ethos that encouraged 'non-bullying' behaviour;
- adequate supervision arrangements and staff being aware of the signs that a child might be a victim of bullying;
- playground design that encompassed a diversity of constructive, creative play with zones for various activities;
- an attitude of mutual trust and respect between children and staff, where staff are aware that children model adult behaviours (Stephenson & Smith 1991)

The Department for Education commissioned a three year research project which surveyed 23 schools in Sheffield (Whitney & Smith 1993). The figures for bullying in the Sheffield survey confirm the degree of 'serious' bullying reported by children in the earlier Kidscape surveys. In the Sheffield survey:

- 27% of the children in junior/middle schools reported being bullied at least once during term time;
- 10% of the children said they were bullied once a week.

ChildLine, the national free helpline for children, ran a telephone line specifically dealing with the issue of bullying in boarding schools. The special Bully Line ran for three months in which over 7000 calls were answered. Notes on 2054 of these calls were written up (Townsend-Wise & Harrison 1991). Bullying for children at boarding school can be particularly difficult because they are not able to escape the bullying by going home at the end of the day.

What is not reflected in these various surveys is the terrible toll that bullying takes on the child and the child's family. Kidscape receives between 200 and 500 letters and telephone calls a week about bullying. Below is a very brief summary of the kinds of problems faced by children and parents.

Case Histories

At last I, like many other people have got someone to talk to, who really understands. I was bullied verbally and it has ruined me. I will soon be 19 but I feel as if I'm only a kid, because I can't stand up for myself. If anyone 'has a go' at me, I break down in tears.

I used to be very fat when I first started secondary school and I was picked on constantly by one of the teachers, in the end I bunked off school more and more, so as well as being picked on by the other girls, I had to cope with bullying from teachers too.

My children have been terrorised, the only word to describe it, for 3 years by the children of one family in our road. Their three youngest boys are aged 5, 8 and 10. My middle two children are aged 7 and 9.

The bullying started as just bad language and threats, escalated to stones, blocks of wood weighing about 2 lb, bricks and tin cans, and culminated two weeks ago in their 5-year-old setting fire to my son's T shirt and burning his chest. As the boy is under 10, the police can't do anything. The Social Services say they 'do not feel it appropriate that we get involved'. The parents thought it was funny, and when questioned by the police insisted that their boys were all indoors watching TV. I saw this incident happen from my window so I know the truth of what happened. The parents aren't of any help, if you go over to them to complain, they shout 'your kids started it' before you even open your mouth. This is followed by bad language and threats. One mum who complained to them was stabbed in the arm with a kitchen knife. She didn't got to the police because the woman told her that her son 'would be next'. After I complained one day that the children had threatened my daughter with a penknife, I was told that if I went to the police my baby would have her face slashed with a razor. The people are council tenants and a couple of us went to the housing office to make a complaint. The council says it is not responsible for the behaviour of tenants and all complaints have to be relayed to the family concerned complete with our names and addresses so that they know who has complained about them. This, of course, would cause more trouble.

My father is nasty to me. People at school leave me out. I used to have some friends who would listen to me and talk, but they started leaving me out and spreading everything I told them. After that I found a new friend, she was someone who had just come to the school. During the week when we had exams she was put with one of my other friends and this other friend didn't want the new girl, so the new girl came to me. She seemed to be a good friend. I never spoke to her about my problems because I didn't know whether I could trust her. Now she has just dropped me and gone off with someone else. I have spoken to teachers about this, but they just say I'll get over it. Things like this have been going on for about two and a half years and it's ruining my life.

Please don't send any information on what I should do before the end of this month because my mum will read it because I'll be on holiday.

I am writing to tell you of my experience of school bullying. I was 13 years old when it started and it carried on until I was 16. It all started because my father couldn't afford to buy me the same clothes as other girls and I didn't have a fancy pencil case. At first it was just nasty comments, then it went to rumours around school of what I was supposed to have done with a boyfriend. Then I mysteriously caught every venereal disease under the sun (or so they said). While all this was going on I didn't tell my dad because I'd only been living with him a couple of years, so I didn't really know him, and was frightened as to who he would believe.

I went regularly to the year-heads, teachers and headmistress complaining about what was happening, but nothing was ever done. I was desperate by this time, I had given the girls' names in and still nothing was done. I wasn't attending school as I was so frightened as to what would happen if I did. Then one day I was beaten up outside school and everyone was yelling obscene names at me, so I thought everyone believed the lies. Of course the teachers blamed me for the fight, although I had gone to the year-head that morning telling the teacher that they were threatening to beat me up after school. I didn't attend school for ages after that and I desperately thought of ways to leave school, although at 15 I knew that was impossible. The straw that broke the camel's back happened one morning. Our teacher was late for registration as usual and the girls in my class thought they would take this time to have a go at me. They approached me and I tried to ignore them which made them worse, so they pinched, kicked and slapped me. I ran from the room knowing it was no good going to a teacher as nothing was ever done.

So to cut a long story short, I went home and in desperation took an overdose. Well, of course, my dad found out what had been going on and thundered up to the school. They did nothing. I did get out of school though. I got pregnant – it was the only way I could see of getting out. I am now happily married with children, but my sister is getting bullied over our mother's death. I have been up to the school, but again nothing seems to have been done. I am so frightened that my sister or other innocents will end up taking such desperate steps as mine. If my overdose had worked, it would have been murder not suicide. And to take the step of getting pregnant to get out of school could have ruined my life, thankfully it didn't, but it did ruin my career. I now have no qualifications and was once a promising student. Please let me help you to make people realise that bullying does exist and is a serious issue.

I am now 19 and have a job, but from the age of 11 to 16 I went through hell both in and out of school. It started when I first went to secondary school. Being brought up with sisters, I was slightly effeminate, quiet and shy, but I had a good brain and IQ. The bullying was mostly name calling and being pushed around. It led to me being absent from school by faking illness but mostly truanting.

I left school with next to no qualifications thanks to being bullied. I could have been doing a degree by now if it wasn't for the hell I had to go through.

The teachers knew and did absolutely nothing; the PE teachers actually joined in with the bullying. I still feel very bitter. It doesn't end when you leave school, the scars and after effects are still there. I have very bad nerves, I have a very bad stomach condition brought on by these nerves and I suffer deep depression and recently tried to commit suicide with pills.

I am a bit better now, but feel that nothing is being done for children like me. The teachers are useless and deny its existence. In this country area bullying is just as bad, if not worse, than in the big cities. I am in a dead-end job having to work my way up the ladder by night school classes and whatever else comes to hand to try and make a success of my life. My scars will never heal and the memories are very strong. I still get the odd nasty name thrown at me, but I have slowly become immune to the hurt I used to feel.

I have heard of you a lot, but never found much about it. I am 8 years old. I would like to know about Kidscape. I have got a problem and would like a bit of advice. I have got a big bully. I am dark-skinned and he keeps calling me names. What should I do?

I am being bullied in school and nobody cares and she has got a gang by her and there just is me and I have got all cuts all over my legs and it has been going on for a long time. It is every day and I just cannot put up with it so I don't know what to do and my mum is in school more times than me and I can't carry on. I should be happy so I want to go to another school if it does not stop everyone just thinks it will just blow over.

There is no one I can talk to, but I hate going to school because everyone is happy except me. A girl at school bullies me. She doesn't hit me or anything like that, but she is very sarcastic and always says awful things. She makes fun of me and how I talk and I end up crying. I am 13 and don't know what to do. Can you tell me what to do to make her stop? It has been going on for months. I don't know why she hates me, but I think she has problems at home. But she is still awful.

My son, now 12, has had a fairly hard time at school – I won't say that some of it isn't his own fault, he's never considered personal safety a barrier to speaking his own mind. But what concerns me most is the attitude of teachers.

At his last school, a highly respected school where parents were assured that bullying was almost unheard of and anyway would be put a stop to immediately if it was brought to their notice, he was teased unmercifully about wearing glasses, 'squint eye' being the favourite term of abuse. I asked my son's year-head if he could put a stop to it – it had taken seven years to get the boy to wear them. He was reassuring and smooth, but his end-of-term comments on my son's report indicated that he must learn to 'watch his mouth' was a trouble-maker and brought all his troubles on his own head. It was, in fact, so hostile that had we not been moving, I would have had to change schools. What bothered me most was that in two years it was the first time it had been mentioned by them. If things were so bad why hadn't they asked to see us?

Mental torture, though, has made school a misery for him. I could cry because I feel so helpless. Please try to get through to the teachers.

Fortunately, attitudes toward bullying are changing and now fewer people think that 'bullying is a good way to learn about life'. Unfortunately, some people still prefer to ignore the problem or, worse, to blame the victims for being bullied. Kidscape school and training programmes and the *How to stop bullying* manual (Elliott & Kilpatrick 1994) help to raise awareness and give practical advice and ways to deal with bullying. We suggest that each school, institution or organisation set out an anti-bullying policy or statement.

There follows an example of the school policy leaflet devised by Kidscape. This leaflet can be adapted and given to parents at the parents' meeting.

Kidscape leaflet: Anti-bullying policy for schools

We are committed to providing a caring, friendly and safe environment for all our pupils so they can learn in a relaxed and secure atmosphere. Bullying of any kind is unacceptable at our school. If bullying does occur, all pupils should be able to tell and know that incidents will be dealt with promptly and effectively. We are a TELLING school – anyone who knows that bullying is happening is expected to tell the staff.

What is bullying?

Bullying is the use of aggression with the intention of hurting another person, and which results in pain and distress to the victim.

Bullying can be:

Physical	pushing, kicking, hitting, pinching or any use of violence
Verbal	name-calling, sarcasm, spreading rum-ours, teasing
Emotional	excluding, tormenting (i.e. hiding books threatening gestures), being unfriendly
Racist	racial taunts, graffiti, gestures
Sexual	unwanted physical contact or abusive comments.

School objectives

- All staff, governors, pupils and parents should have an understanding of bullying.
- Bullying will not be tolerated.
- Clear procedures for reporting bullying should be understood and followed.

Procedures and outcomes

1. Report bullying incidents to staff.

2. In cases of serious bullying, the incidents will be recorded by staff.

3. Parents should be informed (in serious cases) and will be asked to come to a meeting to discuss the problem.

4. If necessary and appropriate, the police will be consulted.

5. The bullying behaviour and threats of bullying must stop immediately.

6. An attempt will be made to help the bully (bullies) change his or her (their) behaviour.

7. The bully will offer an apology and other appropriate consequences may take place.

8. In serious cases, suspension or even exclusion will be considered.

9. If possible, the pupils will be reconciled.

Prevention

We are using Teenscape lessons as a basis for tackling bullying. As and when appropriate, this may include writing a set of school rules, signing a behaviour contract, writing stories about bullying and reading them to a class or assembly, drawing pictures, making up roleplays and having discussions.

Signs and symptoms (from Kidscape's 'Stop bullying!')

A young person may indicate by signs or behaviour that he or she is being bullied. Adults should be aware that these are possible signs and that they should investigate if a young person:

- is frightened of walking to or from school
- is unwilling to go to school
- begins to do poorly in school work
- becomes withdrawn, starts stammering
- regularly has books or clothes destroyed
- becomes distressed
- stops eating
- cries easily
- becomes disruptive or aggressive
- has possessions go 'missing'
- has dinner or other monies continually 'lost'
- starts stealing money (to pay bully)
- is frightened to say what's wrong
- attempts suicide or runs away
- has nightmares

These signs and behaviours could indicate other problems, but bullying should be considered a possibility and should be investigated.

For a free copy of *You can beat bullying*, a guide for young people send a large stamped address envelope to: Kidscape (address in Help Organisations, Unit 4)

Child abuse

Recognising the signs

Unless a child or young person tells, it is difficult sometimes to know if abuse has occurred. Children who have been abused usually show the effects in some way. Below are lists of the signs that have been known to characterise the various forms of abuse. Although these signs do not necessarily indicate that a child has been abused, the possibility should be investigated if a student is exhibiting a number of these or any one of them to a marked degree.

Signs of abuse

Physical abuse

- unexplained injuries or burns, particularly if they are recurrent
- improbable excuses given to explain injuries
- refusal to discuss injuries
- untreated injuries
- admission of punishment which appears excessive
- fear of suspected abuser being contacted
- bald patches
- withdrawal from physical contact
- arms and legs kept covered in hot weather
- fear of returning home
- fear of medical help
- self-destructive tendencies
- aggression towards others
- chronic running away

Emotional abuse

- physical, mental and emotional development lags
- admission of punishment which appears excessive
- over-reaction to mistakes
- continual self-deprecation
- sudden speech disorders
- fear of new situations

- inappropriate emotional responses to painful situations
- neurotic behaviour (e.g. rocking, hair-twisting, thumb-sucking)
- self-mutilation
- fear of parents being contacted
- extremes of passivity or aggression
- drug/solvent abuse
- chronic running away
- compulsive stealing/scavenging

Neglect

- constant hunger
- poor personal hygiene
- constant tiredness
- poor state of clothing
- emaciation
- frequent lateness or non-attendance at school
- untreated medical problems
- destructive tendencies
- low self-esteem
- neurotic behaviour
- no social relationships
- chronic running away
- compulsive stealing or scavenging

The following is an excerpt from *Keeping safe: a practical guide to talking with children* (Elliott 1994).

Sexual abuse

Young people from the age of 12 may:

- hint about secrets they cannot tell
- say that a friend has a problem
- ask you if you will keep a secret if they tell you something
- begin lying, stealing, blatantly cheating in the hope of being caught
- have unexplained sources of money
- have terrifying dreams
- be chronically depressed/suicidal
- exhibit sudden inexplicable changes in behaviour, such as becoming aggressive or withdrawn
- stop enjoying previously liked activities, such as music, sports, art, scouts or guides, going to summer camp, gym club
- be reluctant to undress for gym
- become fearful of or refuse to see certain adults for no apparent reason
- act in a sexual way inappropriate to their age
- be inappropriately seductive
- have urinary infections, bleeding or soreness in the genital or anal areas

- be unable to concentrate
- play truant
- have chronic ailments, such as stomach or headaches
- take over the parent role at home, seem old beyond their years (if victim of incest)
- develop eating disorders, such as anorexia or bulimia
- have a poor self-image, self-mutilate
- be severely restricted by a parent î not allowed to mix with friends or go out with boys (or girls)
- continually run away
- be wary, watchful
- attempt to sexually abuse another child
- talk or write about sexual matters, hoping that someone will discover what is happening

It is important to note that these lists are possible indicators of abuse Many of the signs could have other explanations.

One teacher concluded that most of her class exhibited one sign or another! However, the lists are useful as a reference.

The scale of the problem

According to Department of Health Government statistics (Department of Health 1993), the number of children and young people in England on the Child Protection Registers at 31 March 1991 and 1992, by category under which recorded, were:

Category of abuse as recorded	1991		1992	
	Numbers	%	Numbers	%
Neglect	6,800	15	7,700	20
Physical injury	10,600	23	10,700	28
Sexual abuse	6,000	13	6,600	17
Emotional abuse	2,600	06	2,800	07
Grave concern	21,100	47	12,900	34

Note. The percentages given in the table will exceed 100 because children who are registered in more than one category are counted more than once. If a child has been physically and sexually abused, for example, they will appear in both categories.

What these figures indicate is that large numbers of children in England are being abused and that they are being monitored or cared for by the local authorities. What the figures cannot give us are the numbers of children who are still suffering abuse.

Surveys about sexual abuse

In Britain

A questionnaire about sexual abuse (Baker & Duncan 1986) was given to a representative sample of 2019 men and women as part of a marketing survey by MORI:

- 13% did not answer this part of the survey
- 10% who answered this part of the survey reported being sexually abused before the age of 16
  Of this 10%:
  - 12% of the women and 8% of the men reported sexually abusive experiences
  - 14% reported abuse was within the family
  - 51% reported abusive situations involving no physical contact
  - 44% involved physical contact but no sexual intercourse
  - 5% reported sexual intercourse
  - 63% reported a single abusive experience
  - 23% reported being abused repeatedly by the same person
  - 14% reported multiple abuse by a number of people

From the MORI survey, it can be estimated that approximately 4.5 million of British adults alive today were sexually abused as children. Further it is estimated that a potential 1,117,000 of the children alive in Britain today can expect to have at least one sexually abusive experience by the time they are 15 years old; 143,000 of those could involve abuse within the family.

In 1988, MORI conducted a survey for London Weekend Television's *London Programme* with 664 young people in the south-east between the ages of 16 and 24. The results were shown on the *London Programme* on 13 October 1988:

- 8% (1 in 12) had had a sexual experience before the age of 16 with an adult
- 17% of the abusers were within the young person's family
- 74% of the abusers were outside the young person's family
- 9% of the young people were abused by adults from both inside and outside the family
- 45% of the young people were aged 14–15 at the time of the first incident
- 55% of the young people were under the age of 13 at the time of the first incident
- 33% of them told someone what happened
- 66% did not tell anyone what happened.

Outside Britain

Countries that investigate and report openly about their social problems show similar statistics on child sexual abuse to those in the MORI survey. Some studies in these countries indicate a higher estimate based on reported incidents. The US Department of Health, through the National Center on Child Abuse and Neglect in Washington DC, has compiled reports of *substantiated* cases of child abuse in the United States. In their 1992 Report, 918,263 cases of abuse and neglect were substantiated. Of these, 131, 504 were cases of child sexual abuse (Dept of Health 1992). West German police annually received 20,000 reports of sexual offences against children (Smolowe 1984).

In one US study (Finkelhor 1984), it was found that 19% of women and 9% of men reported sexual victimisation as children.

From this, Finkelhor estimated that between 2 million and 5 million women had been sexually abused as children. Using the same statistics we can estimate that between 1 and 3 million men were sexually abused as children. (In the USA a child is anyone under 18).

Who are the offenders?

Research indicates that offenders are generally immature, manipulative, inadequate and they tend to blame others for their own failings. Many were victims of abuse as children. In one of Nicholas Groth's prison studies of child molesters, it was found that 80% of the offenders had been themselves either physically or sexually abused as children (Groth, Hobson & Gray 1982).

Of the reported cases of child sexual abuse in the UK, 97% were committed by men (Mrazek, Lynch & Bentovim 1981), though more evidence is now emerging about abuse by women.

In one US study of sexual offenders (Abel, Mittlemand & Beczer 1982), it was found that, on average, each offender had:

- attempted 238 child molestations
- completed 166 molestations
- created 75 child victims

It was also found that approximately 30% of the child molesters reported that alcohol increased their sexual arousal to children.

Many of the sex offenders in this study (42%) had deviant fantasies at a young age, some as early as 12 or 13 years old. A way must be found to identify and treat such young people before their behaviour becomes harmful to others.

In the most comprehensive study to date of male sex offenders, sponsored by the Nuffield Foundation (Elliott, Browne & Kilcoyne 1995), it was found that:

- 70% of the offenders had committed offences against 1 to 9 victims
- 23% committed offences against 10–40 children
- 07% committed offences against 41–450 children
- 66% of the offenders knew their victims; 34% were strangers to the victims
- 49% of the offenders were attracted to children who seemed to lack self-esteem
- 48% isolated their victims through babysitting
- 61% of the offenders were worried about the victim telling someone about the abuse

The Nuffield study highlights the importance of alerting parents and other adults to the methods used by offenders and of teaching children assertiveness and to tell if they are asked to keep touching of any kind a secret.

The various studies of offenders seem to show that they do not 'stand out'. Many appear to be normal people leading normal lives. They come from every background, race and social class. Many are married with children of their own. People are usually quite surprised if they find out that someone they know has sexually abused a child. It is difficult to reconcile that anyone who looks and acts normally could be a child molester. This can be a problem when a child or young person reports an incident of abuse. Some adults prefer to think that the child is lying or has manipulated the adult.

Abuse of children and young people by women
It has long been recognised that children are neglected, and physically and emotionally abused by women. It is only recently, however, that the issue of women sexually abusing children has been raised publicly. Although the statistics indicate that the vast majority of reported sexual abusers are male, there is growing evidence from survivors that women also sexually abuse. In a study (Elliott 1993) of 127 men and women who were sexually abused by women, it was found that:

- 25% had been abused by both men and women
- 75% were abused by women acting alone
- 78% said they were not believed when they told about the abuse
- 96% said the abuse had dramatically adversely affected their lives
- 7% of the female survivors admitted sexually abusing children
- 22% of the male survivors admitted sexually abusing children

Who is responsible?
Legally the adult is always responsible for sexual offences against children. See later in this unit for definitions of criminal offences.

Cycles of abuse

Surveys have shown that many offenders have themselves suffered sexual or physical abuse as children. The re-enactment of that abuse on a new generation of children often gives them a sense of power and may be the only way they have learned to interact. It is this cycle that must be broken in order to keep children safe.

This is not to say that all sexually abused children will become offenders as adults. Many children who have been abused grow up to be loving adults and parents.

In summary

The literature indicates that the effects of child abuse can be measured by a range of social ills: alcoholism; drug dependency; suicides; delinquency; truancy. It can also lead to emotional disorders. Far better to prevent the abuse, if possible, than to have children suffer the consequences of child abuse in any form.

Telling/disclosure

As telling an adult is one of the basic messages of good sense defence, it is possible that a young person will tell you about something that has happened to them.

In our experience, the majority of incidents that you are likely to come across will involve bullying, flashing and obscene telephone calls. These experiences can be very upsetting, sometimes to the point of causing nightmares. Talking about the experience and eliciting the help of an adult will obviously be a great relief to the young person. You may also be told about more serious incidents, such as chronic bullying, physical, emotional or sexual abuse or incest. These types of offences are potentially very damaging. For example, incest is likely to have continued over a prolonged period of time, thus creating the worst possible effects in the life of the young person.

Dealing with telling/disclosure

In the case of incidents such as flashers, keep a record in a school log book of those that are reported. You can either use the suggested format we provide in Unit 2 or devise one of your own. Make a note of:

- who saw the incident
- when it happened
- where it happened
- any information that can be remembered which might be helpful.

Information like this can help police to identify patterns in behaviour, which might lead to the person being caught.

In one school, three children from different classes each reported separately that a man was offering children rides in his blue van. By collating the three different reports it was possible to establish what the van looked like and where it was usually parked. Using records of incidents reported is a very direct way of keeping children safe.

It is possible that some of the incidents may be more serious. You will be familiar with your local procedures and what is expected to happen when you report. It is never easy to support a child or young person in crisis – what is often needed is support for the person helping the child. Hopefully you will be given this support, either at work, or at home or from friends.

Criminal Offences

Rape – is forceable sexual intercourse. Consent by a child to intercourse is immaterial. It is not necessary for intercourse to be completed. Penetration to any degree is sufficient. (Section 1(1) of the Sexual Offences Act 1956 as amended by Sexual Offences (Amendment) Act 1976.)

Unlawful sexual intercourse – It is an offence for a man to have intercourse with a girl under 16 to whom he is not married. It is not necessary for intercourse to be completed. Penetration to any degree is sufficient. It is a defence in respect of girls aged 14–16 where:

- there is a marriage invalid under English law
- The man is under 24, has not previously been charged with a similar offence and reasonably believes the girl to be over 16
  (Sections 5 and 6 of the Sexual Offences Act 1956.)

Incest – is sexual intercourse between persons related within certain degrees. Consent is immaterial:

- by women over 16 to have intercourse with a man she knows to be her father, grandfather, son, brother (or half brother).
- by a man to have intercourse with a woman he knows to be his daughter, granddaughter, mother or sister (including half sister).
  (Sections 10 and 11 of the Sexual Offences Act 1956)

It is an offence for a man to incite a girl under 16 to have incestuous sexual intercourse with him. (Section 54 of the Criminal Law Act 1977)

Buggery – Is unlawful sexual intercourse by penetration of the anus. Penetration to any degree is sufficient with a woman, a male under 18 years or a child under 16 years. (Section 12 of the Sexual Offences Act 1956 as amended by Sexual Offences Act 1967)

Assault with intent to commit buggery – This is an alternative offence where the act falls short of buggery, or penetration cannot be proved. (Section 16 of the Sexual Offences Act 1956)

Gross indecency – refers to acts of indecency only between males. Physical contact is not always necessary. Examples of gross indecency are mutual masturbation, and oralÅgenital contact. Offences include committing an act of gross indecency, being party to the commission, or procuring the commission of the act. The word 'gross' has no significance in law. (Section 13 of the Sexual Offences Act 1956 as amended by Sexual Offences Act 1967)

Indecent assault – does not have any formal legal definition but there must be an assault, that is an application of force or hostile act or gesture, and it must be accompanied by circumstances of indecency. It does not matter how minor the assault is if it occurs in circumstances of indecency. Examples of indecent assault are touching a child whilst suggesting an indecent act, and touching the inside of a child's thigh. (Sections 14 and 15 of the Sexual Offences Act 1956)

Indecent conduct with or towards a child – This can be done by any person who commits an act of indecency with or towards a child under 14 or who incites a child under 4 to commit such an act. Examples of this are adults who ask children to touch them or an adult who asks two children to commit an indecent act on each other (provided one child is under 14). (Section 1 of the Indecency with Children Act 1960)

Causing or encouraging prostitution or intercourse with or indecent assault on a girl under 16 – Person committing the offence will be the person having responsibility for the girl. It is sufficient to allow the girl to consort with or enter into, or continue in the employment of a prostitute or person of known immoral character. The implication is that the person must have knowledge of or allow the action to continue. (Sections 25, 26 and 28 of the Sexual Offences Act 1956)

Indecent photographs of children – It is an offence for a person to:

- take or allow indecent photographs of a child to be taken
- distribute or show any such photographs
- have in their possession indecent photographs with a view to their distribution or publication.
- have any indecent photograph of a child in his possession. (Section 160 of the Criminal Justice Act 1988)

Note.
— 'Children' means persons under 16
— 'Indecent' is not defined but will be a matter for the Court
— 'Indecent photographs' includes films and copies of films and

photographs. It also includes negatives and any form of video recording. A single frame of any film is sufficient.

In cases of unidentified children in indecent photographs, the age may be determined by the Court.

Any photograph that portrays a child in an indecent scene, even though the child may not be pictured indecently, is covered by the Act. (Section 1 of the Protection of Children Act 1978)

Implementing Teenscape

We thought it might be helpful to include a time table, which was used in one area when implementing Teenscape. It may be too complicated to gather a cluster of schools using the programme, but the plan is included as a guide, especially for the possibility of disclosure of abuse which may follow some of the lessons.

Start of autumn term

1. Education Welfare Officer (EWO) to send circular to secondary schools to discover which intend to implement the programme during that academic year and to ascertain (rough) proposed date.

Autumn half term

2. Names of schools wishing to participate to be circulated to each other and relevant support agencies.

3. Network for support between participating schools to be set up, for example:

   — by local meeting of headteachers or representative members of staff (respectively for Health Education or Special Needs)
   — by joint Inset for training

4. Staff (teaching and support) to have been allocated adequate time to talk through their own feelings, experiences and anxieties.

December break

5. Schools to advise EWO of their wish to set up the 'professionals meeting' via standardised form, listing appropriate people and functions and details, for example:.

FUNCTION	NAME
Educational Psychologist	_____
Education Welfare Officer	_____
Social services	_____

School Nurse   _____
Schools Liaison Officer   _____
Respite Care Worker   _____
Youth leaders   _____

6. EWO to notify named persons of details of this meeting. (The schools' list of required professionals could be copied and attached to a standardised letter), such as:

    _____ School is planning to implement Teenscape workshops during the _____ term and would like to invite you to a meeting of professionals to discuss support networks and strategies. This will be at _____ on _____ am/pm. In addition, we would like to invite you to a meeting for parents which is scheduled for _____ at _____ am/pm.
      We would greatly appreciate your returning the attached form:

    Name _____ will be unable/able to attend the professionals' meeting at _____ School at _____ on _____

    Please forward minutes of the meeting   ·   YES/NO

    I will contact you re alternative support
    offer   YES/NO

    Parents' meeting date _____ I wish to attend   YES/NO

    One senior EWO to co-ordinate meeting. Minutes to be taken for professionals unable to attend but willing to assist.

7. *Before the professionals' meeting* schools to arrange date for parents meeting.

8. Schools to draw up lists of young people about whom there is concern.
    — on 'child protection' register
    — showing signs of abuse or bullying
    — disclosed by pooled information from professionals
    — worrying because of emotional/social/education problems.

Spring term

9. Workshops and follow-up sessions to be agreed

10. Accurate notes to be kept following any disclosures of abuse.

11. All young people disclosing to be given support and reassurance in school; therefore appropriate teachers must be aware of the situation.

12. All parents (except in exceptional circumstances) to be notified of disclosure by most appropriate agency.

13. Case conferences to be arranged where necessary.

14. Therapy to be arranged where possible and appropriate.

15.   Teachers' involvement to be maximised in monitoring and supporting young people who have disclosed.

End of summer term

16.   All disclosures to have been followed up.

17.   No child to be left unsupported over holiday period.

18.   Programme to have been completed, allowing adequate time for delayed disclosures.

19.   Staff to have decided how the programme will be reinforced and messages repeated to be sure that pupils have fully assimilated the ideas.

Follow-up

20.   Schools Health Education policy and programme to be developed to incorporate this programme so that it is not seen as a 'one-off', and slots appropriately into the curriculum, Multi-disciplinary training sessions to be set up where possible (e.g. for counselling).

21.   Schools to look to ways of producing their own follow-on to reinforce the programme.

References

Abel, G., Mittelman, M. and Beczer, J. (1982) *Sexual offenders: results of assessment and recommendations for treatment*, New York State Psychiatric Institute and the Department of Psychiatry, College of Physicians and Surgeons, Columbia University, New York City.

Baker, A. and Duncan, S. (1986) 'Child sexual abuse: a study of prevalence in Great Britain' *Child Abuse and Neglect*, vol 9.

Department of Health [UK] (1993) *Children and young people on child protection registers year ending 31 March 1992*, A/F92/13, prepared by the Government Statistical Service, p 30.

Department of Health [USA] (1992) *Child maltreatment 1992:reports from the States to the National Center on Child Abuse and Neglect*. US Department of Health and Human Services, Washington DC.

Elliott, M. (1991) 'Bullies, Victims, Signs, Solutions', in Elliott, M. (ed.), *Bullying a practical guide to coping for schools*, Longman, Harlow.

Elliott, M (ed.) (1993) *Female sexual abuse of children: the ultimate taboo*, Longman, Harlow.

Elliott, M. (1994) *Keeping safe, a practical guide to talking with children*, Hodder Headline, London.

Elliott, M., Browne, K. and Kilcoyne, J. (1995) 'Child sexual abuse prevention: what offenders tell us. Nuffield Foundation study' in *Child Abuse and Neglect, The International Journal*, vol 19: 4.

Elliott, M. and Kilpatrick, J. (1994) *How to stop bullying*, Kidscape, London.

Finkelhor, D. (1984) *Child sexual abuse, new theory and research*, Collier MacMillan, New York.

Groth, N., Hobson, W. and Gray, T. (1982) 'The child molester: clinical observations' in *Social Work & Child Sexual Abuse*.

Mrazek, P. B., Lynch, M and Bentovim, A. (1981) 'Recognition of child sexual abuse in the United Kingdom' in Mrazek, P. B. and Kempe, C., H. (eds.) *Sexually abused children and their families*, Pergamon Press, Oxford.

Olweus, D. (1993) *Bullying at school: what we know and what we can do*, Blackwell, Oxford.

Smolowe, J. (1984), 'A rude awakening in Europe', *Newsweek*, 14 May, 1984, pp 36,37.

Stephenson, P. and Smith, D. (1991) 'Why Some Schools Don't Have Bullies', in Elliott, M (ed.), *Bullying, a practical guide to coping for school* Longman, Harlow.

Townsend-Wise, K. and Harrison, H. (1991) 'A child's view Å how ChildLine helps', in Elliott, M. (ed.), *Bullying, a practical guide to coping for schools*, Longman, Harlow.

Whitney, I and Smith, P. (1993) 'A survey of the nature and extent of bullying in junior/middle and secondary schools', in *Press Educational Research*, vol. 35, no. 1.

Unit 2   Planning the Programme

Introduction

This unit explains:

- how to develop the Teenscape programme for teaching young people good sense defence
- which other agencies may be involved
- the objectives of the staff meeting

Good communication between all relevant agencies and a clear understanding of procedures are vital prerequisites to implementing the Teenscape programme. This unit gives suggestions about ensuring that everyone knows what is happening before teaching young people good sense defence. We have found that even a brief meeting can help to eliminate any misunderstandings and that it makes the programme run more smoothly.

Unit 2 is divided into three chapters:

Chapter 1 – First steps
How to set up the meeting with staff and people from agencies outside the school or institution

Chapter 2 – The planning meeting
Gives practical suggestions about how to plan for teaching the lessons and setting up the parents' meeting

Chapter 3 – Teachers' workshops
To give those teaching the lessons a chance to practice their skills

Chapter 1   First Steps

Letting people know

Schools and other organisations have to decide if they wish to have a meeting and, if so with whom. In some schools a small group of teachers discuss the most appropriate way to proceed, in others one person takes the lead. The first step to is identify all the people you feel will need to be informed and/or invited to a meeting. The programme could possibly affect a wide range of people who come into contact with young people:

- Within the school:
  — school governors
  — secretarial staff
  — catering staff
  — maintenance staff
  — transport staff
  — supply staff
  — parent/teacher associations
  — voluntary workers

- Outside the school:
  — police
  — social services
  — health services
  — education welfare service
  — educational psychologists
  — NSPCC/RSSPCC/ISPCC
  — youth workers/play leaders etc.
  — local voluntary organisations
  — respite care organisations
  — local theatre groups
  — organisers of community programmes

This is not a comprehensive list. There may be other people involved with your school whom you feel should be informed of the programme.

You may already have contact with representatives of the organisations listed and have established ways of working together.

The need to know

Forming a team such as the one suggested above is an important step in setting up the Teenscape programme. It ensures that there is a recognised and clearly understood network which you can refer to in the event of a young person from the school being abused or bullied or harmed in any way. In this sense, it is a precautionary measure. There are, however, a number of other reasons why these people need to be involved:

- Concern about the problem of child safety, abuse and bullying has increased over the past few years.
- Different agencies may be planning to tackle or have already tackled the problems in a variety of ways. By letting as many relevant agencies as possible know of your plans, you will minimise the risk of unnecessary duplication or confusion.
- Several agencies may be involved in the procedure established for dealing with incidents. They may be agencies that you want to contact or refer teenagers to.
- There may be agencies or organisations that have existing programmes about which you need to be aware, such as local theatre groups presenting plays about bullying or child abuse and self defence classes that are available.
- A number of people will need to know that the school is teaching good sense defence, in case a teenager or parent reports a case of suspected bullying or abuse to them. Young people can build up 'special' relationships with any of the adults who work in the school. They might choose to tell the secretary or the dinner supervisor or the caretaker about something that has happened to them.
- Teenagers with special educational needs may be unable to tell directly, though they may give clues that they are being abused. If the staff are aware that the young people are being taught good sense defence, they may understand better what a student is indicating or trying to tell.

Some of these people or agencies may be able to help you carry out the programme. They might help with reproducing some of the materials; assisting with the running of the parents meetings; the teaching of lessons, etc.

Invitation list

Having identified all the agencies and groups that you think should be informed of your plans to implement the programme, draw up a list of individuals from those organisations to be invited to a meeting at the school.

Try to make sure that you get the appropriate representative from the larger organisations. If you have the time, it is worth finding out exactly whom to send the invitation to rather than hoping that the letter will get passed on to the right person.

Once you have drawn up an invitation list, you can start planning the meeting itself. There are a number of practical considerations that you will need to decide, most of which you are no doubt aware.

When the meeting will take place – what is the most convenient time?

Where the meeting will take place.

How long the meeting should last – how much time is needed?

Who will lead the meeting on the day – who is the best person in terms of commitment, experience and time to prepare?

Objectives of the meeting

The suggested objectives of the meeting are as follows.

- To inform people about Teenscape and the opportunity it provides to develop a good sense defence programme in the school.
- To learn about any related activity by other agencies.
- To plan, in conjunction with other agencies, a programme for teaching good sense defence in the school.
- To ensure everyone understands the procedures to dealing with cases of bullying, abuse or other problems which may arise.

You may have additional objectives.

What happens in the meeting

The meeting can be divided into four sections:

1. Introduction
2. Information Exchange
3. Teaching Programme
4. Procedures

These sections are dealt with more fully in the next chapter of this manual.

Preparing for the meeting

The following suggestions may help.

- Familiarise yourself with:
  - the background information in Unit 1;
  - what happens in the parents meeting;
  - what happens in the lessons.
- Plan what you want to say in your introduction. This could include:
  - how long the meeting will last;
  - the objectives for the meeting;
  - what will happen in the meeting.
  Further details are contained in the next chapter.
- Identify any problems that you think may arise when you implement the programme in your school:
  - difficulties with fitting it into the timetable;
  - shortage of staff;
  - lack of equipment or resources.
  You can then ask people at the meeting if they are able to help you overcome these problems or if they are in the same boat!
- Clearly establish the procedures with specific reference to child abuse and bullying.

Chapter 2   The Planning Meeting

Introductory talk

As suggested in the previous chapter, it is a good idea for the person who will be introducing the meeting to prepare what they are going to say beforehand.

The talk should be as short as possible, given the busy schedules that everyone has. It might include:

- who you are (if necessary)
- what the meeting is for
- what Kidscape is (see Unit 1)
- the decisions that must be made by the end of the meeting

Ideally, the talk should probably last no longer than 15 minutes. Points for the talk could also be taken from the next unit, which has a scripted meeting for parents. It could be adapted for the planning meeting, if you wished.

Information exchange

It might be a good idea to ask each of the representatives of outside agencies:

- to tell if they are currently involved in any way with the safety of children;
- to explain, if appropriate, the nature of the activity, and how it could relate to the programme.

Any useful information that is obtained from this process can be recorded on a chalkboard or flipchart so that it can be referred to throughout the rest of the meeting.

To ensure that this part of the meeting does not take up too much time (or is taken over by someone who thinks you all want to listen to a long, boring resumé of his or her work), you may want to:

- brief people before the meeting;
- limit the time for each person to three minutes or less;
- discuss at the beginning of the meeting how much time there is for the

entire discussion (and reiterate the 'time limit' for individual presentations);

- record key points on the flipchart/chalkboard while each person talks.

Teaching programme

Two basic decisions need to be made by the meeting before the planning of the teaching programme can progress:

- how best to establish a network that involves all the appropriate agencies/individuals;
- how to ensure that everyone knows the procedures.

The details of the programme can then be discussed. These details involve:

A.   the timetabling of lessons for teenagers
B.   the organisation of meetings for parents
C.   the planning of follow-ups to the lessons
D.   the teaching of the lessons.

A. Timetabling lessons

Details of what is involved in the lessons on good sense defence are contained in Unit 4. When the lessons can best be taught will depend on:

- how they can be fitted into the existing school timetable
- how much preparation time is required by the people teaching the lessons. (The lessons are scripted to save time, but some people may wish to develop their own versions.)

There are two main ways the lesson plans can be used. These are not the only ways, but they will give you some idea of how the plan can be adapted.

1.   The lesson plans are set out in sections. The length of the lessons is suggested, but this depends upon the ability and concentration levels of the young people you are working with, and on how much discussion you encourage/allow The lessons cover:
     — Introduction
     — Trusting intuition
     — Saying no
     — Feeling safe
     — Safety when out
     — Dealing with bullies
     — Crime
     — Rights and responsibilities
     — Relationships

— Abuse
— Getting help/telling someone
— Keeping safe from abuse
— Common sense defence
— Addiction
— Gambling

2. More than one lesson could be taught in one block, if necessary, though it will take longer than the suggested time to complete and might be more difficult to take in.

Whichever approach you choose initially, it is recommended that provision be made for some follow-up activities and lessons. This will ensure that the messages are repeated and reinforced. It can be done by including secondary activities that fit into your continuing work with a particular class or by using the suggestions at the end of lessons in Unit 4.

Timetabling of the lessons will depend on what approach you decide to use. It will also depend on the size of group you wish to teach. We recommend that each class be taught on its own, but it is possible, if necessary, to teach the lesson to larger groups of young people.

B Parents' meeting

Details of the organisational requirements of the parents' meetings are contained in Unit 3. Some decisions need to be made now though:

• Whether it is necessary to call a parents' meeting or if you will send home notices about the lessons without holding a meeting.
• Whether to arrange one meeting for all parents, or to arrange a series of smaller meetings for different groups of parents (e.g. based on a tutorial group).
• When to arrange the parents' meetings. The meeting should take place as close to the first lesson as possible. If it is feasible, both the parents' meeting and the first lesson should take place in the same week, so that the contents of the meeting are still fresh in parents' minds when their children come home after the lessons.
• Who will run the parents' meeting and who will attend. One arrangement that has proved very successful is a combination of the headteacher and those will be teaching the lesson. The availability of these people will obviously bean important factor in the scheduling of the parents' meetings.

Planning the parents' meetings might result in some slight alterations to your timetabling of the lessons. When you have completed both to the group's satisfaction, ensure that everyone has a copy of the time-table.

C. Follow-up

There are a number of ways in which you can follow-up the lessons to reinforce teaching points and see how much the young people have remembered:

- Use the suggestions at the end of the lessons.
- Put up a copy of the anti-bullying rules suggested in the bullying lessons in every classroom.
- Post a copy of the school questionnaire completed in the bullying lessons and discuss it in assembly or class meetings.
- Re-teach key elements of the lessons at different points throughout the term.
- Invite individuals from one or more of the outside agencies represented in the meeting to come into the school to explain their work if this is appropriate (and doesn't already happen). If you do this, however, make sure that this will not result in teenagers receiving confusing or contradictory messages.
- Use the young people's own stories and ideas as the basis for roleplay or drama sessions.
- Devise your own, or have the students devise, quizzes, games, crossword puzzles or other activities.
- Do written work or drawing on the theme of bullying.
- Have a poster contest on one of the themes in the lessons and award prizes or certificates.

D. Teaching the lessons

The lessons do not have to be taught only by the school's teaching staff. One of the representatives from your network of agencies may want to be actively involved in implementing the programme in your school. This could include the police, the health services, the social services, education welfare service, respite care workers, voluntary workers, school governors and parents.

Kidscape recommends that, ideally, the class teachers of each group of children be involved in teaching the lessons.

The meeting needs to decide who will teach which lessons of the Teenscape programme.

Summary

At this stage in the meeting, you should have decided:

- when the lessons will take place
- when the parents' meetings will take place
- who will be running the parents' meeting
- what kind of follow-up will be provided
- who will be teaching the lessons.

The *Working Together* guidelines were jointly developed by the Department of Health, the Department for Education, the Home Office and the Welsh Office. *Working Together* was devised to give guidance for dealing with child abuse. Ensure that all those at the meeting know about and understand the details of the Guidelines, which are available from the Department of Health.

Procedures

It is important that everyone is aware of his or her own role and responsibilities, and how they are involved in the wider 'network' of agencies/individuals invited to the meeting.

It is also important that all those at the meeting know about the procedures for dealing with bullying. Ensure that your guidelines are written down and clearly understood.

The procedures need to make clear what to do if any of the adults in the school are made aware that a teenager is or has been abused or bullied. This should include:

- who in the school should be given this information and what their responsibilities are;
- how the information should be recorded;
- the contact in the local police force, if necessary;
- the contact in the local social services office, if necessary;
- how to support the young person;
- sources of further support and counselling for staff, as well as for the young person and family;
- telling the family that a teenager can be educated at home, if necessary.

These are all important elements of the school's procedure which should be known by all those involved in the school. It is advisable to have information available about procedures to follow in cases of child abuse or bullying or other issues. It may be a good idea to display these procedures in the staff room.

As well as young people talking about experiences of bullying or child abuse, there may be colleagues who wish to talk about things that happened to them. We have found that talking about good sense defence, particularly as it relates to child abuse and bullying, seems to encourage those involved in running the programme to tell their own experiences. Be sensitive to the possibility that people you work with may have suffered abusive experiences, including bullying, when they were children. Discussing the subject now may prompt them to talk about what happened to them. Allow them the same understanding and time that you would to students or parents. If a colleague wants to talk, ensure that there is a place for privacy and time to listen.

Some suggested guidelines for dealing with disclosures are given in Units 1, 3 and 4.

The planning meeting will have covered some important issues. It might be helpful to those attending it to have a copy of the decisions that were taken.

Does it work?

It is difficult to measure the value of a programme such as Teenscape. We asked one of the headteachers involved in the original pilot study, to give us her thoughts a year after starting the programme.

Running the pilot scheme for Kidscape was at the same time, the most foolhardy and the most rewarding venture our school has undertaken. Like most heads, I was concerned to implement a positive curriculum programme to protect the students in general and to allay my nagging doubts about specific individuals whose problems could not be properly identified or helped by involvement from the usual support services. As a pilot school, we also had the additional anxiety of not being able to predict the response from the students or know the kind of assistance we would need from the support services.

The programme consisted of several parts. There was an initial parents' meeting, explaining that the students would receive an enjoyable positive safety programme – not something to worry or frighten them. Parents were given the outline of the lessons so that they could talk to their children after the lessons to reinforce the messages. Even those whose children were later identified as the victims of bullying or abuse were, after the initial shock, immensely grateful that their children had felt able to share their problems, and that they could now be supported and protected from the situation continuing.

A professionals' meeting was also called to arrange back-up. Teachers agonised long and hard about their own feelings and experiences. However, most of the staff were prepared to take on the lessons and spend the time necessary to teach them. Later, some of the staff offered to break the news to the parents of children in their classes who had revealed problems, which was helpful when they had a particularly strong relationship with a family.

The lessons themselves were lively, positive and good fun. The students were actively involved in all of the lessons, which made the learning much more interesting to them. They did reveal a dilemma between their super-ficial understanding of media coverage – many wanted to talk long and loud about abuse, bullying, rape cases and child murders reported on television but, at the same time, some thought that strangers were 'dirty old men in macs'. They really needed the opportunity to talk, and ask perplexing questions in a non-emotive atmosphere.

After the lessons, they were given the opportunity to come individually to talk if they had any kind of problem – about bullies, abuse, anything at all. Some revelations were trivial. Others were appalling in their severity. The space, time and opportunity to talk was vital. The most important support we could give was to listen sympathetically and believe them. In most cases, they wanted us to tell their parents and make them believe too. We followed up and supported every case. It took a whole year. For me, the point of disclosure was hardest. I found it very difficult to control my own feelings of anger, anxiety and depression at what these children have suffered. I agonised over whether the support was adequate to justify implementing the programme.

At this most depressing point, things suddenly got better. The improvement in academic and social terms of the children with the most traumatic experiences suddenly mushroomed. A student who could write only a few confused words suddenly wrote a coherent story covering three sides of A4 paper. Another student's reading ability improved by three years in a matter of weeks. The rapport with teachers became very close. Children began to use Teenscape strategies for dealing with bullying situations, in the playground. Some began to form their first trusting relationships. Students without bad experiences felt more confident and supportive of each other.

Kidscape has done a terrific job for this school. Our Teenscape manual is the best resource I have. It's all in there, step by step. Any committed school can implement it. The permission to say 'no' won't turn a school into a chaotic madhouse. It doesn't work that way. It's too important to the students themselves.

It does, however, need to be an integral part of a whole school curriculum and health policy. It is a natural extension of all aspects of safety, health and the development of individual responsibility.

The commitment of teachers is paramount and on-going. Although our programme is completed, we are now working on associated areas: setting up a whole school policy on bullying, ensuring that the lessons are rein-forced every year.

By accepting the Kidscape philosophy that a child has a right over his or her own body, you take on the necessity of teaching Teenscape strategies that develop an independent and an assertive attitude. The compliant, conforming student becomes one who is at risk. The ramifications of this project are very far reaching. You can't implement Teenscape without preparation and to commitment, but . . . what price a child's peace of mind?

Chapter 3   Teachers' Workshops

There are three main reasons why it is advisable for the people who will be teaching the Teenscape lesson to meet together beforehand.

1. To increase understanding of and familiarity with the subject of good sense defence.

2. To increase confidence in tackling the subject of child abuse and bullying.

3. To develop the skills and techniques needed for teaching the lessons using roleplay.

All of these objectives will be achieved more easily with the support and feedback available from a small group. This can be extended beyond the workshops suggested here. You may find it useful, for example, to meet together after each lesson to compare notes and discuss ways of improving or following up your performance.

Familiarisation

Knowledge of child bullying and abuse must also include an understanding of the feelings of students who have been involved in such incidents.
   The exercises in this chapter are designed to help you to:

*   familiarise yourself with a child's perspective on getting help in an adult world;
*   develop your approach to teenagers who may have experienced some form of abuse.

Confidence

You may be feeling anxious about dealing with the subject of good sense defence in the classroom; you may be worried about frightening the students or about 'taking the lid off a can of worms'!
   By working in a group beforehand, you can:

*   share any anxieties that you may be feeling;

- talk them through with other people who may be feeling exactly the same;
- be reassured by the feedback of colleagues;
- prepare strategies for dealing with your anxiety, should you have any.

Practice

The plan provided for the lessons in this Manual has been developed, refined and proven successful again and again – the feedback from those using it has been excellent.

To ensure that you also get the best results from the programme, we suggest you look at the lessons as they are laid out in the lesson plan in Unit 4. For instance:

- There may be parts of the lesson that you want to adapt to suit your teaching style.
- There may be techniques, such as roleplay, which you are not familiar with, and will need to develop prior to the lesson.
- You may need to adapt the lessons for young people with special educational needs.
- If you are sharing the lesson with another 'teacher', you will need to co-ordinate each of your contributions. This will require practice to ensure that you don't interrupt each other or have a different understanding of who is doing what.

Workshop activities

This section provides you with activities for a workshop that can be used to increase your understanding of the issues and emotions involved. We recommend that everyone who will be teaching the lessons does the workshop as minimum preparation, though we realise this will not always happen.

The activities should give you:

- a clearer idea of the issues involved;
- greater confidence in teaching good sense defence;
- an opportunity to develop techniques you may want to use in the lesson.

How you organise the activities will depend on:

- who is in the group – for example, you may need to spend some time at the beginning of the workshop getting to know each other better;
- how much time you have – you may not have time to do all the activities in one workshop;
- how much space you have – you may only have room to do the activities that don't require any moving around;

- who is leading the workshop – you may decide to appoint someone;
- how much time you may need to spend discussing issues.

It is best if all the members of the group have an opportunity to read this chapter of the manual before attending the workshop, so that they have an idea of what is likely to happen.

The activities

Some people may not be used to doing activities like the ones listed below. They may feel uncomfortable and embarrassed about taking part. The workshop should give people time to settle in and become more relaxed before any of the activities are attempted.

Assure people that they will not be expected to either perform for or repeat personal feelings to the whole group. This should make them more comfortable when they undertake the activities.

One way of starting the workshop is to ask people a general question that has nothing to do with the teaching of good sense defence.

- Go round the group asking each person to say briefly how they are feeling about doing the workshop.
- Go round the group asking each person what they expect to happen in the workshop, what time they have to leave by, etc.

Spend some time discussing each activity after you have done it. The group can then talk over their responses to the activity and share any memories that it may have evoked.

Activity 1 – How can you say that?
This activity gives you an understanding of the power that adults can have over young people.

- Get into pairs and assume roles as either an 'adult' or a 'teenager'.
- The 'teenager' tells the 'adult' the he or she is being bullied.
- The 'adult' denies this statement: 'No, it's not happening.' 'You've misunderstood – it's only a bit of fun.' 'Don't be ridiculous, we don't have bullying in this school!'
- The 'teenager' tries to convince the 'adult'.
- The 'adult' continues to deny that this is true.
- After a few minutes swap places and repeat the exercise, so that the 'teenager' becomes the 'adult' and vice versa. This time the 'teenager' tells the 'adult' that she or he is hungry and the 'adult' denies that this is true.
- Discuss the exercise with your partner; describe how it felt and whether it brought back any memories of when you were a child.
- In the full group, check whether you ever behave like that to other adults and discuss why you think it is that adults behave to children and teenagers in this way.
- Ask members of the group if anyone can remember a time when they

have refused to believe something a child has told them which later turned out to be true.

- Stress that this exercise gives some idea of how difficult it can be for a child in telling someone that an adult has tried to abuse them in any way; and how important it is to teach children to go on telling people until they find someone who will believe them.

Activity 2 – I've never been so frightened in my life!
This activity explores some of your own childhood memories, and how some memories, though frightening, are remembered almost with affection, whereas others still cannot be laughed off.

- Return to the pairs established for the previous exercises.
- Each person is given three minutes to tell of an occasion when he or she was frightened as a child or teenager. The story should begin with the words: 'I have never been so frightened in my life!' The partner must not interrupt or say anything until the story has finished.
- When the three minutes are up, the person listening repeats the exercise, telling a true story beginning with the words 'I have never been so frightened in my life!'
- When the second story has finished, the first story-tellershould return to his/her own story, and tell the partner whether:
  — the memory still upsets him/her;
  — the incident became a family joke;
  — it became the basis for a fear that stayed throughout childhood;
  — he/she told anyone about it or kept it a secret.
  The partner can now ask questions to help the story-teller describe how he/she feels about the incident now.
- This should then be repeated with the second partner's story.
- Discuss in the full group whether adults take into account the impact that events like these can have on a child's life. Look specifically at how adults react to children who have undergone a frightening experience: do they respect children's feelings or do they belittle children in the belief that this will help them 'get over it'?

Activity 3 – Points of view
This activity is a roleplay of a young person telling about a bullying or abusive experience. It gives you experience of what it is like for a child to tell someone about an incident of bullying or abuse, and an opportunity to practise listening techniques.

- One person plays the 'child', another plays the 'teacher'. A third person watches the interaction and gives feedback to the other two at the end of the roleplay.
- The 'child' has been the victim of a bully (or an obscene telephone call or a flasher). He or she has asked to see the 'teacher' after class.
- The 'child' tells the listener about the bullying or telephone call or flasher. The 'child' wants to tell, but is frightened of what will happen

– the consequences of telling might make the situation worse. The listener is encouraging, asking open-ended questions, if possible, and helping the 'child' to tell.

- The 'child' and 'teacher' act out the scene, watched by the observer, who does not interrupt.
- The observer halts the scene after five minutes or when it is not useful to continue it and gives feedback to the 'actors' about what he or she saw happening, i.e. by describing the scene enacted as closely as possible.
- Repeat this exercise so that all three people have a chance to perform each role at least once.
- In your threesome, discuss the activity in some detail, focusing on:
  — how you felt as the child and as the teacher;
  — what you learned about the 'child';
  — what you learned about dealing with a child telling.

Incident log

The incident log can be used to to record cases of bullying and reported abuse. Check with your local education authority to ensure that you are following your local procedures. A sample log form is opposite.

Incident log form

. . . . School

INCIDENT LOG

. . . . .Date

Date of incident. . . . . Time of incident. . . . .

Person reporting. . . . .

Address . . . .

. . . .

Telephone . . . . Relationship to school . . . .

Details of incident . . . .

. . . .

. . . .

. . . .

. . . .

. . . .

. . . .

Referred to . . . . On (date) . . . .

Action taken . . . .

. . . .

. . . .

. . . .

Person completing report   Signature

. . . .

Person witnessing report   Signature

Unit 3   The Parents' Meeting

Introduction

This unit suggests ways to organise and run the meeting for parents.
The purpose of the parents' meeting is:

- to explain the Teenscape programme;
- to explain why you want to teach good sense defence to their children
and how they can reinforce the messages at home;
- to answer their questions.

Kidscape has found that the most effective way of teaching prevention
techniques is by enlisting the support of parents and carers wherever
possible. Throughout Unit 3 we refer to parents. 'Parents' here means
any adult or adults with whom the child is living and who are
responsible for the child's welfare îguardians, foster parents, residential care workers, etc.

Unit 2 is divided into three chapters:

Chapter 1 – Making contact
The steps that need to be taken to set up the parents' meeting.

Chapter 2 – Running the meeting
Step-by-step plan of what to do in the meeting itself. It includes a
scripted talk which can be used as is or become the basis for a talk to
parents.

Chapter 3 – After the meeting
Deals with possible issues that may arise from the meeting – questions,
need for reassurance or advice that might be voiced by parents.

Chapter 1   Making Contact

At the planning meeting, you will have decided:

- how many students are going to be involved in each lesson;
- when the lessons will be taught;
- who is teaching the lessons.

These decision may affect how you set up the parents' meeting:

- you may have one large meeting for all the parents;
- separate meetings for the parents of all the students in one year;
- separate meetings for each class.

Letter and leaflets to parents

At the end of this unit, we provide a model letter (from which you can design your own) to send to parents, which notifies them of the meeting.

Also at the end of this unit, we include two leaflets (see further details below) which can be adapted as appropriate either to send home with the letter or to be handed out at the parents' meeting. Of course, you may wish to design your own or prefer not to give out information in this form. Knowing (from personal experience as a teacher) how little time you have, we are just trying to make it as easy as possible by giving you something as a basis.

Once the letters have been reproduced, they should ideally be posted to the parents. They could be given to students to take home but this creates an obvious risk.

Hopefully, most parents will return the slip indicating that they intend to come to the meeting. It is probable that some parents will not respond to the letter at all. You will have to decide if you have the time and resources to:

- ring any parents who have not sent back the return slip;
- send home another copy of the letter with a hand written note explaining that you would appreciate their response.

If parents either don't respond or can't come to the meeting that you have arranged, you may try to organise another meeting for those parents if the numbers warrant this and if you have time.

Time and place

When

The parents' meeting should, if possible, be organised in the same week that you plan to begin teaching the Teenscape programme. If this cannot be arranged, try to ensure that the parents' meeting happens as close to the first lesson as possible, so that the information is still fresh in parents' minds. This makes it easier for parents to reinforce the messages at home.

Where

Where you hold the meeting will depend on how many parents are coming. You will know best what rooms you have available to hold different size groups.

- The smaller the room the better, as long as there is room for everybody! Smaller rooms make for a more relaxed atmosphere.
- If possible, have drinks available for people as they come in. This will help them relax and give them something to focus on while they wait for the meeting to start.
- It can also be useful to provide drinks at the end of the meeting, as it encourages an informal atmosphere at a time when parents may wish to talk to you.

Handing out leaflets

If you choose to hand out the leaflets at the meeting, it gives parents something to focus on if they don't know anyone else or are a bit shy.

One leaflet, entitled *Good Sense Defence* explains the basics of the Teenscape programme to parents. The other leaflet, entitled *Child Abuse*, gives signs and symptoms of child abuse. There is a third leaflet in Unit 1 which is a model of a whole school anti-bullying policy. You may wish to use any or none of these leaflets.

Plan of meeting

The plan of the meeting in the next chapter includes a framework for a talk to be given at the beginning of the parents' meeting. This framework is based on the model used by Kidscape and thousands of schools in the many presentations given to groups of parents over many years. The talk should last no longer than 15–20 minutes.

The framework provides all the necessary information to be included in the talk. Whoever gives the talk may need to spend some time preparing it prior to the meeting, as suggested below.

- Read through the framework provided.
- Decide how best to use the framework. Some examples of ways it could be used include:
  — exactly as it is scripted;
  — as notes for you to refer to during the meeting;
  — as the basis for a speech that you write out before the meeting;
  — as the basis for a talk that you improvise during the meeting.
- It might be a good idea to practise giving your talk before the meeting, so that you can sort out any problems that you may not have anticipated.
- try the talk out on friends or friendly colleagues well before the meeting. They will be able to give you feedback on whether the presentation is clear. Their reaction may also give you some idea of how parents are likely to react and the possible questions they may ask at the end of the meeting.

Summary

A summary of the main messages that are taught in the lessons is included at the end of the talk and in the *Good Sense Defence* leaflet.

Chapter 2   Running the Parents' Meeting

This chapter of the 'parents meeting' unit is a step-by-step guide to running the meeting itself.

The meeting consists of three main parts:

- an introductory talk;
- summary of the lessons;
- a question and answer session.

What needs to be done?

A number of tasks are involved in running the meeting. We suggest that, if possible these tasks are shared amongst a number of people who will run the meeting. They will need to:

- hand out leaflets for parents at the beginning of the meeting, if you decide to give out the leaflets;
- give the introductory talk;
- summarise the lessons;
- invite and try to answer the parents' questions.

What does Teenscape *provide?*

- leaflets for parents;
- an introductory talk;
- a summary of the lessons;
- a list of questions commonly asked by parents, and suggested answers.

After the meeting

Some parents might want to speak to you after the meeting or arrange to come to see you at a future date. The third chapter of this Unit gives guidelines for dealing with such possibilities.

Feelings about the meeting

Most, if not all, of the parents attending the meeting will be pleased that the school has taken the initiative of setting up the good sense defence programme. However the whole subject of children's safety can engender strong feelings, particularly the issue of child abuse and bullying.

Parents attending the meeting may be feeling curious or apprehensive about the meeting ahead.

It is also a possibility that some of the parents might themselves have been bullied (or were bullies!) or have had abusive experiences.

It is important, therefore, that the meeting starts off on the right foot. Parents will need to be made to feel comfortable and relaxed as soon as possible. They will need to be reassured that the meeting isn't going to be 'difficult' or embarrassing.

As people come in

- Try to make contact with each person as they come through the door.
- Hand a copy of the leaflet(s) to every parent as they come in. As not everybody will arrive at the meeting at the same time, the leaflets will give them something to focus on if they don't want to make contact with other people.

Making a start

When you are ready to start the meeting, make sure someone stays by the door to welcome any latecomers, hand them the leaflet(s) and show them to a seat.

In starting the meeting:

- thank everybody for coming;
- introduce yourself;
- introduce any members of staff present;
- introduce anyone attending the meeting representing an agency or organisation involved in the programme;
- make sure everybody has the leaflet(s).

When everybody is ready, explain what is going to happen during the meeting:

- that you are going to talk for 15–20 minutes;
- that you will summarise the lessons;
- that you will then try to answer any questions that they might wish to ask – you might prefer that people save their questions until the end;
- that, at the end of the meeting, you will give out a form for parents to fill in to indicate that they consent to their child being involved in the lessons;
- that you will stay behind for a specified amount of time after the meeting to see any parents who might want to talk with you.

Before you start the introductory talk, make sure that everybody can see and hear you clearly.

We have broken down into note form the text of the talk. These notes are either a 'read it to them' text or a framework from which you can devise your own presentation.

Talk for parents

Introduction

We are here to talk about how to help keep our children safe from all kinds of dangers. We want to know how, as parents and concerned adults, we can take action to help children learn to keep safe.

When I use the term 'parent', I am, of course, talking about anyone who is acting in a parental role.

I think we would all agree that childhood should be a time of fun and discovery, but part of the process of discovery for children must include learning how to deal with potential dangers.

- *Teenagers are confronted with many different situations.*
- *Most children, at some stage, will find themselves in a frightening situation, such as getting lost, or being bullied by another child, or perhaps by an adult.*
- *Young people need information about how to keep safe and how to get adult help.*

We are using a concept called 'good sense defence'. This has been created by the children's charity Kidscape as a method of teaching children positive and practical ways to help them stay safe. Thousands of teenagers, parents and teachers in schools in the UK and abroad have used this programme successfully.

'Good sense defence' depends for its success on the active involvement of everyone in the community who cares about children.

Bullying

Let's start with a problem that is unfortunately not rare – bullying.

- *Bullying is a problem many children have faced.*
- *In the first nationwide survey on bullying, Kidscape found that 68% of the 4000 children in the survey said they had been bullied. Unfortunately, bullying is a widespread problem.*
- *It is probable that many adults here have also been bullied as children – in fact, some adults are bullied as adults, at work or even at home.*
- *Some adults are also bullies.*
- *Bullying is a problem that has always been with us, but this school is trying its best to ensure that the children here are not bullied.*

If you have given the parents a copy of the anti-bullying policy, say:

You have been given a copy of the anti-bullying policy we have developed with the help of students, staff, parents and governors. Please take it with you and let us know if you have any suggestions. We have tried to make the policy fair and we ask your co-operation to help make this school safe from bullying. Obviously this is not the time or place to discuss individual cases, but contact us after the meeting if you would like to arrange a private appointment.

In the lessons we will deal with bullying by using discussions, questionnaires and drama to get the children involved and to help them realise that bullying is wrong and that it hurts people. The important messages are that no child deserves to be bullied and no child should be a bully. We also tell teenagers that, if you see someone being bullied or know that someone is being bullied, you have an obligation to try to help or tell an adult what is happening. We know we can't solve all problems overnight, but we think this programme will help.

Approaches by strangers

- *The thought of a child or teenager being abducted makes us all shudder.*
- *In a survey by Kidscape of 1000 parents, 98% of parents living in cities said that the threat of a child being abducted was their biggest worry; 96% of parents living in country areas expressed the same fear.*

This image that many people have of the outside world as hostile and threatening to children is obviously one parents share to some degree but, before we try to keep our teenagers home or forbid them to go anywhere or do anything more exciting than playing video games, we do need to examine the accuracy of the image.

According to the Home Office Statistical Bulletin (Issue 9/93), over a five year period ending in 1991, 35 children between the ages of 5 and 15 were killed by strangers. This average of 7 deaths a year, though quite small, is still 7 deaths too many. However, there are over 12 million children in the country so we must take care not to over-react to the threat of child abduction. We do not have a figure for the numbers of children abducted by strangers and then returned, as those case records are kept on a local, not national basis. We do know that there are many more of these cases than there are child murders. I will come back to that in a few minutes.

Having said that, we feel it is important that teenagers continue to not to talk to strangers when they are on their own and certainly not to go off with anyone, (teenager or adult), they don't know. Not talking to people they don't know when they are on their own may help them avoid potentially dangerous situations. The difficulty is that teenagers think they are invincible and that nothing can happen to them. We still need to reinforce the idea that they should beware of going to that party where they don't know anyone or going off with someone they met in a disco. The danger for teenagers is that they often have the bodies of adults and so look as though they can take care of themselves, but they don't have the life experience to go with it. They definitely still need our guidance.

Sexual assault by strangers

Earlier I said I would come back to the issue of abductions that do not end in the murder of a child or teenager.

- *The statistics, again from the Home Office, on sexual assault of children or young people under the age of 16 present a different picture from that of abduction.*
- *Some 12% of rapes of children or young people under the age of 16 are committed by people not known to them. For teenagers the assailant may be that person they met once at the disco, who seemed so nice – until he or she got the teenager alone.*
- *Between 20% and 24% of sexual assaults on children under the age of 16 were committed by strangers.*
- *Therefore children are more at risk from sexual assaults by strangers than they are from murder by strangers – still not a very comforting thought.*
- *We must remember that the numbers are still not very great – approximately 6000 recorded victims – compared to the 12 million children in the UK. But we need to ensure, as much as possible, that children do not become victims of sexual assaults by anyone, including strangers and people known to them.*

Sexual assault by people known to the child or teenager

- *There is a far greater threat to children or young people than sexual assault by strangers, and that is sexual assault by people known to them.*
- *Remember that 12% of rapes of children or young people under the age of 16 are committed by strangers – which means that 88% are committed by someone they know.*
- *If 20–24% of sexual assaults of children or young people under the age of 16 are committed by strangers, this means that approximately 75–80% of this abuse is done by someone they know.*
- *It is hard to imagine anyone harming a child or teenager in this way but unfortunately it does happen.*
- *Before you become concerned, be assured that Teenscape does not frighten teenagers about relationships. The whole approach is low-key and non-sensational. The emphasis is on talking about how touching, kissing and hugging should never be kept secret. Secrecy is the key to sexual abuse – the abuser tells the child not to tell, and so the abuse goes on.*
- *Teenscape teaches young people to tell if anyone asks them to keep touching a secret, even if the touching feels good, as it sometimes does.*

- *Teenagers are also encouraged to tell if they are being physically abused. This is done by saying that 'we see in the news sometimes that children are beaten or starved or burned'. In this way we distance the abuse for most young people, unless they recognise themselves as being beaten, starved or deliberately burned. Then, of course, we want to know so we can help.*

Perhaps brief definitions of abuse would help determine what we are talking about.

- *Sexual abuse includes:*
  — *indecent assault*
  — *rape*
  — *buggery*
  — *fondling*
  — *oral sex*
  — *incest*
  — *taking pornographic photographs.*
- *Physical abuse includes:*
  — *beating*
  — *hitting with belts, brushes, whips etc.*
  — *burning*
  — *pinching, twisting ears, biting.*
- *Children and young people are also emotionally abused by being told continually that they are worthless, stupid, ugly or a great burden, and so on.*
- *Children and young people may be neglected by not being fed, clothed or properly looked after.*

The Teenscape programme explains this to teenagers; however lessons explain that most adults would not harm children or young people, although some people do have problems. These people might touch or hug or kiss a child in a way the child doesn't like, or that is uncomfortable, or that might even feel good. Then that person tells the child not to tell anyone. The message is that if anyone, even someone you know, does this, tell someone you trust, preferably an adult, and keep telling until someone helps you.

How widespread is the problem?

- *Approximately 10% of British men and women have had sexually abusive experiences as children. These statistics come from a representative MORI poll.*
- *From these figures it has been estimated that a potential 1,117,000 children in Britain today can expect to have at least one sexually abusive experience before the age of 16.*

So it is important that children learn to tell us when they feel frightened, worried or uncomfortable about touching. We just may prevent some children having to go through the horror of abuse.

A few final points. We should be aware that children will experiment, both alone and with other children the same age, as a way of learning about their own bodies.

- *It is natural for children, at all ages, to explore their own bodies. This should not, in itself, cause alarm.*
- *It is important that we don't over-react, and start looking for instances of sexual abuse everywhere!*

One mother mistook a game of doctor and patient that her young daughter and a friend were playing as sexual assault. The older child was only using the stick as a pretend thermometer!

We must find a way of helping children to keep safe. They must be given ways of recognising potential danger without making them fearful of all adults.

- *Young people must be taught to trust their own instincts, but they need hugs and kisses and should not be made distrustful of normal, everyday affection. Understanding the difference between open, loving hugs and kisses and those that are furtive, forced or tricked enables children and young people to trust their own feelings and to seek adult help.*
- *Teenagers must be taught that it is OK to say no to an adult who asks them to do things that don't feel right.*
- *Teenagers must be taught to tell another adult if someone is trying to force them to keep secrets.*
- *Teenagers must be taught, in such a way that enables them to use their own judgement, to help protect themselves.*
- *By ensuring that adults believe and help young people, we can begin to reduce the problems of bullying and child abuse.*

Tell parents of the steps that the school is taking (as agreed at the planning meeting), which may include:

- keeping an incident log;
- establishing procedures with the police and other agencies;
- when the lessons will begin;
- plans for any follow-up lessons later in the year.

Tell parents about other agencies that are co-operating in the programme.

Lessons summary for parents

Now you may wish to summarise the lessons that are described in Unit 4, using the key points listed below. You may wish to expand on them or describe in more detail the way in which your school intends to run and present the lessons. Remember that there is a summary of the lessons in the leaflet for parents, 'Good Sense Defence', so you might choose instead to invite parents ask questions about the lessons.

The lessons

- **Introduction** – setting up ground rules and ensuring that the students are supportive in discussions.
- **Trusting intuition** – learning to trust the feeling that says 'don't do this' or 'get away now' or 'I don't like this situation'. Teenagers often get into difficulty because they are too embarrassed to say 'no' or to leave.
- **Saying 'no'** – the students are taught to say NO and get away, if possible. They are not taught to threaten an abuser or attacker that they will tell – a potentially dangerous thing to say, which might provoke an attack on them.
- **Feeling safe** – students are encouraged to think of where and with whom they feel safe.
- **Safety when out** – using a series of 'what If?' questions, students think of strategies for keeping safe when out with friends or alone.
- **Bullying** – several lessons are included in this section helping teenagers to deal with bullying and to encourage them to get help if they are being bullied.
- **Crime** – using a list of crimes, the students discuss how they view crimes and what their ideas are for stopping crime.
- **Rights and responsibilities** – using roleplay and discussion, the students look at issues such as under-age drinking, helping elderly neighbours, football hooliganism, bullying and other topics to think about what responsibilities they have in various situations.
- **Relationships** - teenagers look at relationships and what they expect from friends or girlfriends/boyfriends. Two questionnaires, designed for young and older teens, are used.
- **Abuse** – the problem of child abuse is looked at through newspaper clippings, definitions and discussion.
- **Getting help** – suggestions about where teenagers can get help for various problems are researched by the students and a list of agencies and organisations is compiled.
- **Keeping safe from abuse** – students are asked to break into small groups and come up with lists of who they think abusers are, who victims are, and where and why abuse happens.
- **Common sense defence** – students are taught a few very simple basic 'getting away' techniques, such as how to get away if someone grabs them, as well as basic rules for staying safe such as avoiding out of the way places and hitch-hiking.
- **Addiction** – this lesson provides an introduction to the problem of addiction and can be used as a springboard for further study of drug and solvent abuse.
- **Gambling** – the problem of gambling, signs and symptoms, and where to get help are discussed in this lesson.

Questions

Tell parents that you will now try to answer any questions that they want to ask. Remind them that you are staying behind after the meeting and will be happy to see anybody who wants to talk with you then.

The section 'Common questions from adults', which follows in Chapter 3 of this unit, gives a list of questions we have often been asked by parents. We have provided suggested answers to these questions for you in preparation for the meeting.

It is impossible to predict all the questions that might be asked. If you are asked a question to which you don't know the answer, say that you will find out and get back to them. You might be able to find the answer elsewhere in this manual. Alternatively, you could refer them to one of the local organisations that were represented at the planning meeting.

When there are no more questions, thank people for coming and close the meeting.

Chapter 3   After the Meeting

The meeting usually provides parents with all the information needed. Some of the parents who attended the meeting may think of issues that need clarifying, or questions that need answering, some time after the meeting has finished. Some parents may have felt unsure about speaking in a large group. For others, the meeting may have brought up personal concerns and they may need further reassurance.

Hopefully we will have anticipated most of the questions that you are likely to be asked. These are given later in this chapter, under the heading 'Common questions for adults. If you are confronted by a request that you can't meet, don't fudge! Either contact one of the local agencies that are involved with the programme, or suggest that the parent contact them direct. Of course, you can ring Kidscape and we will do our best to help.

Overload!

How you deal with parents after the meeting depends on how much time you can afford to give to such demands. It is important that you don't create problems for yourself by responding to more demands than you can cope with.

To avoid being overloaded, make full use of the network of local agencies and people who are involved with the programme.

Disclosures from parents

Having presented the issues raised at the meeting, it is possible that some parents will recall past experiences from their own childhood during general conversation with you after the meeting has ended. It is often these experiences that will lead to a very positive and supportive reaction from parents to the programme.

You might find that a parent may be seeking an exclusive or private opportunity to talk to you. This may be because:

- they suspect or know that their (or another) child is being abused or bullied;
- they themselves were abused or bullied in childhood.

If you receive any confirmation that either of these circumstances is likely, first consider whether it is the most appropriate time and place for dealing with the situation. You may need to arrange another opportunity to continue the discussion.

Below are guidelines for dealing with the eventuality of abuse.

Suspicion or knowledge of child abuse

- Tell them that you cannot promise to keep secret what they tell you if it involves the safety of children.
- Explain the procedure for dealing with such incidents.
- Make sure that they understand to whom you will pass on the information that they give you, if this is the course you need to take.
- Ask them if they still want to tell you.
- Ask them if they want to contact the authority to which the school has decided to relay such information.
- If they do, ask them if they would like your help to do this.
- If they don't, tell them that you will contact the authority on their behalf or on behalf of the child.

Disclosure of past experience

- Ask them if the offender is still likely to be abusing children.
- If the answer is yes, go through the steps outlined above.
- Let them know that you understand how difficult it is to talk about such matters.
- Encourage them to speak, but try not to make judgements about what they are telling you.
- Ask them if they want to talk to someone now that they have told you.
- If they do, refer the person to the organisation that you have identified during the planning meeting.

Although you are not expected to be a therapist, just listening to someone who wants to tell you of a personal experience may be enormously helpful to them. In fact, that is all most people want to do. Many survivors of child abuse have related that being believed and supported by the first person they told was very important.

Common questions from parents and suggested answers

Does talking about prevention frighten children?

We already warn children from an early age about the danger of going with strangers, but have seldom given them the kind of information they need to keep themselves safe, especially from abuse by people known to them. Ask any group of teenagers about the kind of messages they have received and they will tell you of their fears.

Giving children ways to help prevent abuse makes them more aware and safe. It is a great relief to children that they are not being given yet more scare tactics and 'don'ts'. Good sense defence gives positive ideas and children enjoy learning how to stay safe. Children who know preventative techniques are not only less at risk because they are informed, but they are also more confident about themselves.

Will children lose trust in all adults if they are taught to say 'no' to people they know?

Children are only taught to say 'no' to touches, hugs or kisses that confuse or frighten them, or ones that are asked to be kept secret. There is never any reason to ask children to keep touching secret. Learning that they can say no and get help if someone forces or tricks them into furtive touching does not affect their trust in adults.

Won't children begin to refuse all kinds of affection?

Children are naturally affectionate, but should be allowed to choose to whom they will give their affection. If someone is making a child confused or uncomfortable with unwanted touching, hugging or kissing, the child should have the right to say no and get support to do this. Learning about good sense defence does not make children less affectionate, and it often makes them even more comfortable about their own bodies.

Won't teaching children to say 'no' make them disobedient?

Children are taught to say no only to uncomfortable or confusing touching. This is certainly not a licence for unruly children!

Isn't it better to say nothing or just concentrate on warnings about strangers?

Children have been left vulnerable for generations by lack of knowledge or warnings only about strangers. As 75% of child sexual abuse is from someone the child knows, this warning is not enough. It is like teaching them to cross the road and only watch out for the red cars. According to the MORI survey, potentially 1 in 10 children will be subjected to a sexually abusive experience before the age of 16, so saying nothing is certainly not an effective method of protection.

Isn't it optimistic to think that children can always be kept safe?

Of course it would be unrealistic to think that. Unfortunately, there will always be circumstances in which children and teenagers will be harmed by determined attackers. But children can be taught with the help of their parents and teachers, to think about ways to keep themselves safe and to act to do so.

As it is, we do not give children enough information so that they can think for themselves. We teach children always to do exactly what any adult says. If an adult tells a child to get in a car, or touches them inappropriately, children often obey without question. Even if they feel instinctively that they should not.

The message that good sense defence gives is that children can do anything necessary to stay safe, including breaking rules, and that we as adults will support them. What we are trying to do is to minimise children's vulnerability.

Isn't there a danger that trying to resist might make the situation worse?

It is not possible to foresee what could happen in every circumstance. Once a child is in a dangerous situation, it is difficult to predict the outcome. That is why it is important to alert children to the potential dangers before it is too late to do anything. For example, yelling to attract attention, when getting help is still possible, makes sense. How will anyone know that a child needs help if the child does not somehow attract attention?

Teaching children to trust their feelings, and to recognise and anticipate dangers, encourages them to protect themselves before the situation gets out of control.

What about violence from the adult known to the child?

The child may feel frightened of the adult. That is why children are taught several strategies, including telling after the event, if that should prove necessary.

Does all this mean I have to be afraid to touch children?

Good hugs, kisses and touches teach children better than any other way the difference between furtive, forced or tricked touches and normal everyday affection. However, adults should always be aware that sometimes children (and adults) do not want to be touched. For example, many children report that they hate being patted on the head or tickled.

No child should ever be forced to be affectionate with anyone, even parents or relatives. This gives the child conflicting messages about being able to say 'no'. 'Kiss Aunty goodbye – go on, silly! Do it!' How often do we force children into situations because we are embarrassed? Then what happens when a molester comes along and says, 'Don't be so silly – do it!'

Do children lie about abuse? We know that they have active imaginations.

Children rarely lie about being abused, so they should be taken seriously. They usually do not have the language or experience to falsely describe abuse. Children may later retract an accusation of abuse for fear of the consequences of having told or to protect someone. Also, because of the traumatic nature of events, details might be confused. Often children make up excuses for bruises so that no one will know they are being abused. In some cases of incestuous abuse, a child has accused someone other than the offender because he or she is too frightened to name the family member. This usually becomes obvious to an expert dealing with the child. However, the fact remains that the abuse occurred.

Occasionally a child can be coached by an adult into saying abuse has occurred, for example in a divorce case. If this ever does happen, the child has not made it up; rather he or she has been forced or tricked by an adult. This is abusive to the child.

There have been a few cases where a child or teenager has made a malicious accusation against someone to 'get even' or get the person into trouble. These cases are tragic for the wrongly accused and the damage done should not be underestimated. The child or teenager obviously needs help, but should also take responsibility for his or her actions, if possible. The consequences may include the child being excluded from school or even that a prosecution is brought.

Why all the interest in child sexual abuse? Is it on the increase?

Child sexual abuse has only recently been discussed in public so we do not know if it is increasing. We know it has been going on since earliest times but we are only now addressing the issues. We do not know all the answers, but the increased awareness and public discussion are beginning to lead to a better understanding of the problem.

If it happens so much, why all the fuss? Maybe it's normal.

We are only now discovering the long-term effects on the victims of child abuse. Child abuse is not 'normal'. It is a crime against children.

Lock up the offenders!

It is often suggested that longer sentences for offenders would solve the problem of child abuse. It is true that some offenders will always be a danger to children and should therefore have long sentences that will keep children safe from them. There are, however, some offenders who are motivated to change their behaviour and who may benefit from treatment. In some of these cases, prison may be counter-productive. Alternatively, the threat or reality of a prison sentence can help to motivate the offender to change.

The real difficulty is that we are still learning how to treat the offenders. Research currently going on in the UK and other countries should lead to a greater understanding of these issues and how to deal with them.

Aren't children sometimes provocative and therefore responsible for what happens?

Children are affectionate and seek adult attention. They are not seeking to be sexually abused. Children can be sensual, but it is the adult who puts a sexual connotation on the behaviour.

Sometimes children who have been abused will turn to adults in a sexual way because that is the only way they have been taught to gain affection. In any case, it is always up to the adult to act in a responsible way to protect and not to exploit the child.

What are the long term effects of child abuse?

It can lead to alcoholism, drugs, mental illness, prostitution, suicide attempts and abuse of future generations. It often produces feelings of guilt, anger and self hatred. The effects are still being uncovered.

Are children with special educational needs at risk?

All children are at risk and should be taught good sense defence to the best of their ability to understand. The techniques of saying 'no' and getting help can be understood by most children.

Do all children who are abused grow up to abuse their own or other children?

No, there are many adults who experienced sexual, physical or emotional abuse as children who have become loving parents and would never harm a child.

Won't talking about keeping safe make children who are already being abused or bullied feel worse?

Children who have been victims are usually relieved to find out that they are not the only ones that this has happened to. It gives them options which they might not have known about, particularly the option to tell. It does not mean that they will necessarily tell immediately, but they will know that it is possible. Often they must find the right time to tell.

What about teenagers experimenting in a sexual way with themselves or with other teenagers?

Teenagers do experiment sexually with themselves and with other teenagers. This should not generally be cause for concern. If, however, a teenager is trying to get younger children to act in sexually explicit ways or tricking or forcing other teenagers or children into sexual acts, this should be investigated. It is possible that the teenager will need help to prevent him or her becoming an abuser.

What is a 'significant age' gap between children in terms of playing doctor or experimenting sexually?

This is not easily agreed upon because young people mature at different levels. Generally for children between the ages of 12 and 16, three or four years difference is significant.

Should adults talk to unaccompanied children?

Although most adults know that they are not strangers intent on harming children, children do not know that. If we teach children not to talk to people they do not know and then we ask children for directions or just chat to them, we do children a disservice. How are they to know that we mean them no harm?

   Most well-meaning adults do not approach children who are on their own and start a conversation with them. Obviously, if a child is in distress and needs assistance, this is a different matter.

What can we do about children being bullied?

Please let the school know if this is going on, providing as much information as possible, such as dates, times, names, etc. Allow some time for the problem to be investigated, and then make contact again. Bullying is not something we tolerate at this school.

Will I make it worse for my child by telling the school?

Staff in school have a legal responsibility to protect your child while in our care. We cannot sort out the problem if we are not aware of it. We will do everything in our power to give the child help and support and to ensure that telling does not make it worse.

What can the school do about bullying?

We have an anti-bullying policy [*you may have given the parents a copy of the leaflet in Unit 1*]. We will try to help and support the victim of bullying and the bully by talking to them separately in a calm and supportive manner. Through the Teenscape lessons we help the children develop coping strategies, such as telling, sticking together and not allowing any of their classmates to be bullied. Most importantly, we will deal with bullying as a school discipline problem and not blame the victim for the bullying.

Bullying has always gone on – it never really hurt anyone. Why bother with it?

Yes, bullying has always been with us, but attitudes are changing. In times past, children have been stuffed up chimneys and down mines and it was considered all right. We know now that bullying does hurt people and can cause enormous grief for children which can last throughout their lives. We are determined that children in this school will not think that bullying in any form is permissible.

I don't want my child involved.

We will make sure that you child either joins another class or goes to the library or [*whatever the school has decided*] during the lessons. Please see me after the meeting and we will arrange it.

I would like my child to discuss the bully and strangers, but not the known adult.

If the school is having separate lessons on each section, this is not difficult. However, if it is only one lesson, work out whatever you feel best for the child.

Shouldn't all these issues be dealt with by parents at home?

Yes, and at school and in the community as a whole. Effectively teaching young people good sense defence should be a co-operative undertaking with parents, teachers and all other members of the community. No one individual or group can be expected to do it alone.

Letter to parents

Dear Parent,

We are planning to involve our students in the Teenscape 'Good sense defence' programme.

This programme is the result of a very successful two-year pilot study in schools in Britain. To date, over 2 million children, and their parents and teachers have taken part in the Kidscape programme, which has been designed to teach children and young people practical, positive ways to help them stay safe.

Teenagers are taught strategies about how to keep safe while out and about, to tell if they have a problem, what to do if threatened by bullies, approached by strangers — or even by someone known to them who might try to harm them.

The success of the programme depends upon the co-operation between parents, teachers and the community. Knowing that you may want to hear more about the issues, we have arranged a meeting on. . . . . at. . . . . p.m. in the . . . .

In addition to teachers and parents, we have invited representatives from organisations that will be involved in the programme.

So that we can plan for the meeting, we would greatly appreciate your detaching and returning the slip below.

We look forward to seeing you.

Yours sincerely,

. . . .

I will/will not be able to attend the meeting for parents

Name . . . .

Name of child(ren) . . . .

Signature . . . .

Kidscape leaflet: 'Child abuse'

Child Abuse – Signs and Symptoms

Although these signs do not necessarily indicate that a child has been abused, they may help adults recognise that something is wrong. The possibility of abuse should be investigated if a child shows a number of these symptoms, or any one of them to a marked degree.

Sexual abuse

- Being overly affectionate or knowledgeable in a sexual way inappropriate to the child's age.
- Medical problems such as chronic itching or pain in the genitals, venereal diseases.
- Other extreme reactions, such as depression, self mutilation, suicide attempts, running away, overdoses, anorexia.
- Personality changes such as becoming insecure or clinging.
- Regressing to younger behaviour patterns such as thumb sucking or bringing out discarded cuddly toys.
- Sudden loss of appetite or compulsive eating.
- Being isolated or withdrawn.
- Inability to concentrate.
- Lack of trust or fear of someone they know well, such as not wanting to be alone with a babysitter or child minder.
- Starting to wet again; day or night/nightmares.
- Become worried about clothing being removed.
- Suddenly drawing sexually explicit pictures.
- Trying to be 'ultra-good' or perfect; over-reacting to criticism.

Physical abuse

- Unexplained recurrent injuries or burns.
- Improbable excuses or refusal to explain injuries.
- Wearing clothes to cover injuries, even in hot weather.
- Refusal to undress for gym.
- Bald patches.
- Chronic running away.
- Fear of medical help or examination.
- Self-destructive tendencies.
- Aggression towards others.
- Fear of physical contact – shrinking back if touched.
- Admitting that they are punished, but the punishment is excessive (such as a child being beaten every night to 'make him study').
- Fear of suspected abuser being contacted.

Emotional abuse

- Physical, mental and emotional development lags.
- Sudden speech disorders.
- Continual self-deprecation ('I'm stupid', 'ugly', 'worthless', etc).
- Over-reaction to mistakes.
- Extreme fear of any new situation.
- Inappropriate response to pain ('I deserve this').
- Neurotic behaviour (rocking, hair-twisting, self-mutilation).
- Extremes of passivity or aggression.

Neglect

- Constant hunger.
- Poor personal hygiene.
- Constant tiredness.
- Poor state of clothing.
- Emaciation.
- Untreated medical problems.
- No social relationships.
- Compulsive scavenging.
- Destructive tendencies.

Note.

- A child may be subjected to a combination of different kinds of abuse.
- It is also possible that a child may show no outward signs and hide what is happening from everyone.

Suspected abuse

If you suspect that a child is being abused, seek advice from the police or social services. It is preferable that you identify yourself and give details. However, if you feel unsure and would like to discuss the situation in confidence, ring the National Society for the Prevention to Cruelty to Children (NSPCC) Helpline, or the Royal Scottish Society for the Prevention of Cruelty to Children (RSSPC) or the Irish Society for the Prevention of Cruelty to Children (ISPCC). You can speak to these organisations (and the police and social services) anonymously. Guidance on finding the telephone numbers is given at the end of this leaflet.

Knowing how damaging abuse is to children, it is up to the adults around them to take responsibility for stopping it.

Telling – disclosing abuse

If a child tells you about abuse:

- Stay calm and be reassuring.

- Find a quiet place to talk.
- Take seriously what you are being told.
- Listen, but do not press for information.
- Say that you are glad that the child told you.
- If it will help the child to cope, say that the abuser has a problem.
- Say that you will do your best to protect and support the child.
- If necessary, seek medical help and contact the police or social services.
- If your child has told another adult, such as a teacher or school nurse, contact them. Their advice may make it easier to help your child.
- Determine if this incident may affect how your child reacts at school. It may be advisable to liaise with your child's teacher, school nurse or headteacher.
- Acknowledge that your child may have angry, sad or even guilty feelings about what happened, but stress that the abuse was not the child's fault. Acknowledge that you will probably need help dealing with your own feelings.
- Seek counselling for yourself and your child through the organisations listed or through your own contacts.

Where to get help

You may consider using the school as a resource, as the staff should have a network of agencies they work with, and will be able to give you advice and/or telephone numbers.

You can contact official agencies or self-help groups. If you are concerned about what action may be taken, ask before you proceed.

The following can be contacted through your telephone directory:

- police
- social services
- Samaritans

(The following numbers are in the Help Organisations Section, Unit 4):

- National Society for the Prevention of Cruelty to Children (NSPCC) in England, Wales and Northern Ireland
- Royal Scottish Society for the Prevention of Cruelty to Children (RSSPCC)
- Irish Society for the Prevention of Cruelty to Children (ISPCC)
- ChildLine

For a free copy of the leaflet 'Why my child?' which helps parents deal with the sexual abuse of their child, send a large SAE to Kidscape (address in Help Organisations Section, Unit 4)

Kidscape is a registered charity founded in 1984 with the aim of teaching children, their parents and other concerned adults ways of keeping children safe.

Kidscape registered charity number 326864

Teenscape leaflet: Good sense defence

'Good sense defence' for young people

Teenscape has been developed to help young people become better able to recognise and deal with a variety of potentially dangerous situations from bullying to coping with strangers or even known adults who might try to harm them.

The Kidscape Programmes, including Teenscape are based upon a two-year project involving parents, teachers and children in selected schools across Britain. Following the success of this pilot scheme, over 2 million children in schools throughout the country are using the programme. Kidscape is a registered charity founded in 1984 with the aim of helping to make children and young people safe. The Kidscape programmes were written by Michele Elliott, child psychologist, teacher and mother of two sons.

By emphasising the positive, and teaching in a low-key, non-frightening way, Teenscape helps young people to stay safe; to understand that no-one – bullies, strangers or people they know – has the right to harm or mistreat them.

Good sense defence depends upon and involves parents, teachers, social workers, education welfare officers, youth workers, police – and all other concerned adults – for its successful integration into everyday life.

The lessons for teenagers cover a wide variety of topics dealing with personal safety. Below is a brief summary of the lessons.

- **Introductory lesson** – setting up ground rules and en-suring that the students are supportive in discussions.
- **Trusting intuition** – learning to trust the feeling that says 'don't do this' or 'get away now' or 'I don't like this situation'. Teenagers often get into difficulty because they are too embarrassed to say 'no' or to leave.
- **Saying 'no'** – the students are taught to say NO and get to away, if possible. They are not taught to threaten an abuser or attacker that they will tell – a potentially dangerous thing to say which might provoke an attack on them.
- **Feeling safe** – students are encouraged to think of where and with whom they feel safe.
- **Safety when out** – using a series of 'what if?' questions, students think of strategies for keeping safe when out with friends or alone.
- **Bullying** – several lessons are included in this section helping teenagers to deal with bullying and to encourage them to get help if they are being bullied.
- **Crime** – using a list of crimes, the students discuss how they view crimes and what their ideas are for stopping crime.
- **Rights and responsibilities** – using roleplay and discussion the students look at issues such as under-age drinking, helping elderly

neighbours, football hooliganism, bullying and other topics to think about what responsibilities they have in various situations.

- **Relationships** – teenagers look at relationships and what they expect from friends or girlfriends/boyfriends. Two questionnaires, designed for young and older teens, are used.
- **Abuse** – the problem of child abuse is looked at through newspaper clippings, definitions and discussion.
- **Getting help** – suggestions about where teenagers can get help for various problems are researched by the students and a list of agencies and organisations is compiled.
- **Keeping safe from abuse** – students are asked to break into small groups and come up with list of who they think abusers are, who victims are, and where and why abuse happens.
- **Common sense defence** – students are taught a few very simple basic 'getting away' techniques, such as how to get away if someone grabs them, as well as basic rules for staying safe such as avoiding out of the way places and hitch-hiking.
- **Addiction** – this lesson provides an introduction to the problem of addiction and can be used as a springboard for further study of drug and solvent abuse.
- **Gambling** – the problem of gambling, signs and symptoms and where to get help are discussed in this lesson.

For more information

Available from Kidscape

For children:

- *The Willow Street kids: it's your right to be safe* by Michele Elliott. Written for junior age children, it answers children's questions and will help them to learn to keep safe in a variety of situations.
- *Bullies meet the Willow Street kids* by Michele Elliott. The Willow Street kids stick together and deal with bullies, with the help of parents and teachers.
- *Feeling happy, feeling safe* by Michele Elliott. Written for young children, this colour picture book gives parents a fun way of teaching children what to do in case they get lost, or are confronted by bullies, strangers or known adults who may try to harm them.
- *The Willow Street kids: on the trail* video shows the Willow Street Kids coping with bullies, attempted abduction and burglars.

For parents, teachers, social workers, trainers and professionals

- *Keeping safe, a practical guide to talking with children* by Michele Elliott. Gives ways of talking to children about keeping safe.
- The **Kidscape** manuals – Primary, Under-Fives and Teenscape, all for use in schools.

- *Protecting children, a training guide for front-line carers* by Michele Elliott. Sponsored by the Department of Health, this manual gives practical advice and exercises for helping children who have been abused.
- *Bullying, a practical guide to coping for schools* by Michele Elliott (ed.). A collection of practical ideas for dealing with bullies, victims, setting up whole school policies, etc.
- **Kidscape** training courses – Provide in-depth training in prevention of child sexual abuse.

Free Leaflets
Send a large stamped addressed envelope to Kidscape for a copy of:

- *You can beat bullying*, a guide for young people for 12- to 16-year-olds.
- *Keep them safe* for parents of 5- to 11-year-olds.
- *Stop bullying!* for 5- to 16-year-olds and their parents.
- *Why my child?* for parents of children who have been abused.

Kidscape registered charity number: 326864

Unit 4   Teenscape Lessons

Introduction

There are 15 lessons in Unit 4. They are self-contained and each can be used independently. However, it might be a good idea to use Lesson 1, Introduction, to set the groundrules for all future lessons. The lessons can be taught by any adult working with young people. They are designed for use with groups of young people, in schools, youth clubs or institutions. The time suggested is just that – a suggestion. You will obviously tailor the lessons to suit your students and the amount of time you have available.

All the initial resources you will need for the lessons are provided, with the exception of paper for the students to write on. The questionnaires, leaflets and lists can all be used as the basis for materials for the students, but not for any other purpose without written permission.

1. Introduction

2. Trusting intuition

3. Saying 'no'

4. Feeling safe

5. Safety when out

6. Bullying
   6a. Questionnaire and suggestions
   6b. Bullying leaflet
   6c. 'Bully courts'
   6d. Journal about bullying

7. Crime

8. Rights and responsibilities

9. Relationships

10. Abuse

11. Getting help

12. Keeping safe from abuse

13. Common sense self-defence

14. Addiction

15. Gambling

Chapter 1   Introduction

Purpose:	To set groundrules for Teenscape lessons
	To encourage students to talk
Time:	40–60 minutes
Materials:	Large pieces of paper and felt-tip markers, chalk-board or flipchart

There are two issues in this introductory lesson. The first is to set up groundrules that will be helpful in all of the work done with students in the Teenscape lessons. The second is to begin to address the feelings the students may have when discussing emotive subjects such as abuse or bullying.

It is important that the issue of groundrules be sorted out first to ensure that the students feel comfortable and safe when sharing feelings. Depending upon the amount of time available, you may wish to divide the lesson into two parts and teach it on different days.

As with all the lessons, we provide a script, which you may wish to use virtually as is or change it to suit your teaching style and the ability of your students.

Groundrules

During this term, we are going to be exploring the issues around personal safety and how to say 'no' and get help in difficult situations. These situations can cover a wide range of topics such as bullying, crime, physical, emotional or sexual abuse and perhaps some ideas on self-defence.

Some of the things we talk about could be embarrassing or painful or cause you to laugh. The lessons will involve some roleplaying, stories and discussions, with many of the ideas coming from you. So I would like to ask your help setting up some groundrules for all of our lessons and discussions about personal safety. When we have a list of groundrules, we will discuss them and then agree on which ones we will follow as a class.

If you have confidence that you can discuss any topic of interest to students (and the governors wouldn't object) you could also have the students brainstorm topics that would be of interest to them. But do not give them the opportunity to do this unless there is a chance to follow through or it will be a pointless exercise. You could also give them the topics listed for the lessons and ask them to tell you of their particular interests or concerns or have them break the topics into sub-groups.

> *We are going to break up into small groups in a moment to brainstorm, but perhaps it would be helpful if I gave you one or two examples of ground-rules.*
>
> *Let's say we are discussing the problem of bullying and there is someone in the class who is either a bully or a victim. I would like to see a groundrule which says that we will not name people or make jokes at anyone's expense, and if there is laughter it will not be directed towards someone else.*

This might translate into two groundrules.

Write on the board: GROUNDRULES

1.   Not to embarrass others.

2.   Not to make fun of anyone.

Decide how you are going to divide the class (i.e. groups of six, eight, mixed groups of boys and girls, single sex, self-selecting, etc.).

> *Would you now get into your groups and ask one person to be your scribe or secretary. That person will write the group's ideas on this large piece of paper in big letters.*
>
> *After you have thought of and written down your ideas for groundrules, we will put up the sheets of paper so that everyone can see what each group has written. You will have five minutes, so think fast and put down as many ideas as you can during that time.*

Give each group a large piece of paper and a felt-tip marker.

It may be that your students will need more or less time to brain-storm. When the students have completed the groundrules sheets, bring them together as a large group and have each group put up their ideas.

As the groups share their ideas for groundrules, write them on the board (or have a student do this) without comment. It usually works better if you take one idea from each group and then go around again. Otherwise, one group may give all the ideas and the other groups will get bored or restless.

When you have recorded the groundrules, decide which ones are agreeable to everyone. One class listed the following groundrules:

—   Not to embarrass others
—   Not to make fun of anyone
—   Allow time to talk
—   No put-downs
—   What is said in the lessons is confidential
—   To be supportive of others

— No-one is allowed to talk for more than two minutes at a time
— No-one to act like a jerk
— No violence
— Class votes on whom to invite in to speak
— Teacher willing to talk privately to students, but not able to promise confidentiality ifhe or she thinks the student is at risk.

This last groundrule was suggested by the teacher, who in this case was willing to spend the extra time. You will need to decide that for yourself.

When the groundrules are agreed, have someone make a poster-type list which is posted. This is the class contract. The groundrules exercise may be useful when you are dealing with issues about bullying and making a school contract in Lesson 6. In fact, you may find these groundrules useful for all lessons, not just for Teenscape.

You may want to agree a plan in case someone breaks the groundrules. What consequences will follow? One class decided that anyone who broke the rules would be made to write up ideas about the lesson and present them to the class. You may decide to exclude someone from a lesson, but there is always the possibility that the student is reacting because the issue hits too close to home.

Feelings

The second task is to deal with the feelings that may arise from discussing emotive and embarrassing issues. We suggest that you ask the students to go back into their groups and make another list of possible feelings that may arise while talking about the Teenscape lessons. Provide them with a list of the topics in the lessons (either on the board or on handouts).

Ask that they again appoint a scribe and come up with a list in five minutes.

We are now going back into the same groups to brainstorm about the types of feelings that may come up when discussing some of these topics. For example, when talking about bullying, some people may feel angry, others may feel scared. When discussing other subjects such as 'Safety when out', if you have had the experience of being mugged or beaten up, you may feel sad, miserable, furious, powerless, etc. So there are many different ways of reacting to these issues.

Write down some of the possible feelings on the board to give the students a model. Have them go back into their groups and give them five minutes to brainstorm.

Allow more time if the exercise is bringing out productive discussion. When they have finished, again make a list of possible feelings, taking one or two initially from each group. The list might read:

—   Angry
—   Hurt
—   Fearful
—   Happy
—   Sad
—   Disgusted
—   Mean
—   Furious

It is important to make a collective list so that the students will know that it is all right to have these feelings and that it is normal. It sets the tone for the work to follow in the other lessons.

There are feelings that many people have when talking about some of these situations. Some people react differently to the same situations. For example, one person might be furious if his or her little brother were beaten up and another might feel happy. It will be important as we talk about personal safety and all the issues to recognise your feelings and talk with someone about them. You may want to think of whom you could talk to, like a gran or mum or dad, a friend, a teacher, etc.

Here you must again decide if you want to be available for the students for private or small group talks. Students will choose their confidants, but sometimes it is comforting to know that a teacher or youth worker or another adult has made the offer of listening (without promises of confidentiality).

The list of feelings is not necessarily to be posted. The purpose is to bring the idea of expressing them into the open. You may wish to continue the discussion by asking the students to think of acceptable ways to express feelings. When going through the lessons, there will be opportunities to turn feelings into positive steps. For example, if students are angry about bullying, there are ways to come to grips with the problem by turning the anger into action such as setting up bullying arbitration courts.

In our next session we will be talking about feeling safe and how our intuition or instincts might help us to keep safe.

Chapter 2   Trusting Intuition

Purpose: To help students learn to trust their own common
                  sense
Time: 30–45 minutes
Materials: Paper, chalkboard or flipchart

*Often the ability to keep safe depends upon trusting those feelings that we
call intuition. Can you give me an example of trusting your intuition?*

If no-one has any suggestions, offer an example such as:

*Michael went out with some friends to the cinema. As Michael and his
friends were walking home, a group of older boys came towards them. Even
from a distance, Michael could see they were drunk and looking for trouble.
He had the feeling that if he and his friends didn't do something, there was
going to be a fight. If he trusted that intuitive feeling, what do you think he
should do?*

Ask the class to brainstorm answers and write them on the board
without comment. Have the class divide into discussion groups to
decide which of the answers they think would work in a real-life
situation. Bring the class back together when they have had sufficient
time and agree on strategies that might work. These may include:

— crossing over the road
— going into a cafe or some other place to get off the street
— going back to the cinema.

One way to help teenagers to think about strategies is to get them to
dramatise the situations. Having determined some possible strategies
to keep safe and trust their intuition, ask the students to roleplay. If
you have three possible solutions, you may want to add another way
to deal with the problem, such as confrontation.

Remind the class of the groundrules. If a groundrule was not made
about physical violence, bring the issue to the attention of the students
and agree to no actual physical violence during the dramatisation. It is
possible, that students will roleplay situations that involve violent
situations to problems. If this happens, allow time for discussion to
explore what would happen if a violent course of action were
employed and the possible consequences.

Divide the students into four groups and give them ten minutes to produce a two-minute roleplay. Have each group present to the class and discuss.

Another method is general class discussion. Ask the class if any of them has ever been in a situation in which they followed their intuition to stay safe. Depending upon the students, you could also ask if there was a time when they didn't follow their feelings, and ask what about the resulting consequences. There is a danger that a child could get upset when relaying such a story or even that a disclosure of abuse could result, so use this question with caution.

Follow-up activities

- Write fictional stories.
- Write about personal experiences.
- Conduct a survey.

A survey

Ask other students about situations in which they have trusted their intuition to help themselves. Ensure that the identity of those responding to the survey is anonymous. Ask only for positive examples to avoid embarrassment. There could be an optional question about times when students did not follow their intuition and the consequences, but this would have to be handled with care.

A sample questionnaire might read:

Have you ever been in a situation in which you listened to your own intuition to get away or keep safe?

_____ YES   _____ NO

If yes, could you briefly describe the incident?

. . . .

. . . .

. . . .

. . . .

What do you think might have happened if you had not trusted your intuition?

. . . .

. . . .

. . . .

. . . .

Optional question

Have you ever been in a situation which your instincts told you was wrong or dangerous and you did not follow your instincts to get away or get help?

_____ YES _____ NO

If yes, can you explain what happened?

. . . .

. . . .

. . . .

How might it have been different if you had followed your intuition?

. . . .

. . . .

. . . .

Compile the results of the questionnaire/survey and publish it for students' use. Ensure that any details which could identify students are disguised so that no repercussions fall on anyone who has taken part. This type of exercise may help teenagers to think carefully about following their intuition if they are ever be in a difficult situation. Stories from peers often make a bigger impact than a lecture from an adult.

Chapter 3   Saying 'no'

Purpose: To teach students assertiveness and that they do
                 have the right to say 'no' if someone is harming them
Time: 20–40 minutes
Materials: Copies of the 'what if?' questions (or they can be read
                 out) from the end of this lesson.

Ask the students:

> *Do you sometime find it difficult to say 'no'? Perhaps you can think of a
> time when it was difficult to say 'no', even though you wanted to. It could be
> any time in your life. For example, when you were younger, did you ever
> have to kiss someone goodbye at the end of a visit? Or did you have to stop
> watching a favourite television programme in the middle because dinner
> was ready? Or did you have to say 'yes please' to some food you didn't really
> want?*

For young people with special educational needs, there may be
additional issues such as having offers of help they don't want, but are
too polite to refuse, or being touched too roughly while being helped,
as well as all the other issues around the right to say 'no'.

Either carry on with a class discussion or divide the students into
small groups. Ask:

> *Can anyone think of a particular incident when they wanted to say 'No, but
> couldn't?*
>   *How did you feel?*

**Be sure to emphasise that it is not always possible to say no, and
that often a person may have no choice but to go along with something they don't understand or don't really want to do. This happens
to most people at some time in their lives. It is important to discuss
this so that no one in the group begins to feel badly because he or
she could not say no, perhaps in a situation where abuse has been or
is occurring.**

If the students are in small groups, ask them to choose one of the
shared experiences and roleplay it, but they must do it without words.
Present the roleplays to the class and see if the rest of the students can
understand the situation.

It would be a good idea to check with each group to ensure that they are not presenting a roleplay that is too personal to anyone or that would not be appropriate for your group.

Discuss the body language of not being able to say 'no' – dropped shoulders, unhappy faces, fear, etc.

Discuss that there are times when it might be impossible to say 'no' – when the situation is too dangerous or the person is too frightened or confused. (See the Follow-up section at the end of this lesson.)

Then ask the groups to talk about how it would have been different if they could have said 'no'. Roleplay the same situations with the students being empowered to say 'no', again without words.

Discuss the differences. If you choose to have a class discussion instead of a roleplay, ask for positive experiences and compare the difference in feelings between the situations.

Activities

Ask the students to divide into pairs. Have one walk like a victim or someone who cannot say 'no'. The others should follow the 'victim', but act assertively and walk confidently. Stop the activity after a minute and reverse the roles.

Discuss the difference in feelings of walking and acting like a 'victim' and walking confidently.

If you were looking for a victim, which person would you approach?

Ask the students to pretend that they dislike cooked carrot and turnip pie. (Or ask the students to suggest something.) Tell them that you are going to feed them this for lunch, unless they can convince you that they don't really want it. Ask them to say 'no' as a group, in response to your statement 'I am giving you a delicious cooked carrot and turnip pie for lunch'. If the first 'no' is not assertive enough, have them stand up and shout 'No', using appropriate body language. Be sure to warn your neighbouring teachers!

Ensure that the students yell 'No' from the stomach, not from the throat. Have them take a deep breath and feel the yell come from the stomach.

Follow-up activities

As a follow-up, ask the students when they think it might be appropriate to yell 'No' and when it might be better to remain silent. For example:

- What if you were in an isolated place with a person who had a weapon and he or she said 'I'll kill you if you scream'?
- What if you were being bothered by a drunk on a crowded bus?

- What if a teacher asked you to do your homework?
- What if someone were bullying you on the playground?
- What if you were home alone and a burglar broke in?
- What if you were on the school bus and someone picked on you?
- What if someone you knew tried to kiss or touch you and you didn't want him/her to, but you were frightened for your safety?
- What if you saw someone being mugged and there are people nearby?
- What if you were being beaten up by a gang of bullies and you could see people in the distance?
- Your brother or sister is driving you mad asking to borrow your Walkman?

Ask the students to come up with other 'what if' type situations so that they can begin to anticipate what strategies they might use.

Chapter 4   Feeling Safe

Purpose:	To help students think about places and people that are safe for them
Time:	30–60 minutes
Materials:	Paper to write up survey questions

There are several ways this session can begin. One way would be to ask the students in a large group discussion when and where they feel safe. Another would be to have them break into discussion groups as in Lesson 1 and ask them to come up with a list. Perhaps the most active and engaging way would be for the students to divide into groups of six and come up with ideas about feeling safe and then have them roleplay one or more of their ideas to the whole group.

If you decide on a group discussion, the following are some possible questions to get the discussion started.

- When do you feel safe?
- Where do you feel safe?
- With whom do you feel safe?
- Are there places or times or people with whom you do not feel safe?

Activities

Depending upon the age of your students, you may want to extend this into making posters or writing stories or doing roleplays. You could ask the students to write a fictional story of a child who felt unsafe. This could bring up sensitive issues which would need follow-up as some students might use the story to tell of their own fears.

It might also be possible for some students to carry out a research project with other students or parents or teachers/staff about attitudes towards personal safety at and around school or when the students are out on their own. For all young people, including those with special educational needs, this exercise could bring up concerns they have about being out in the community or about bullying (see Lesson 6 about bullying). A graph of responses could be organised and posted in the school. One school survey looked something like this:

Tick 'Safe' or 'Unsafe', according to how you feel.

	Safe	Unsafe
Do you usually feel safe or unsafe:		
on the school playground/fields?	_____	_____
coming to and from school?	_____	_____
on the school bus?	_____	_____
in the lunchroom?	_____	_____
in the toilets?	_____	_____
in the classroom?	_____	_____
in the corridors?	_____	_____
in the library?	_____	_____
in the changing rooms?	_____	_____
by the bicycle sheds?	_____	_____
at the school gates?	_____	_____
on school journeys?	_____	_____
with other students?	_____	_____
with staff?	_____	_____
I usually feel?	_____	_____

The list can be changed or modified for your particular group of students. One school compiled and graphed some of the responses to their survey for a maths class:

Students in this school say they feel safe:

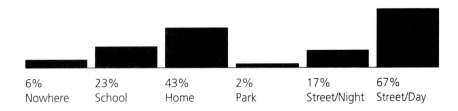

6%	23%	43%	2%	17%	67%
Nowhere	School	Home	Park	Street/Night	Street/Day

Points to stress

- Everyone has the right to be safe – children, young people, parents, teachers, police, old people.
- No-one should take away your right to be safe.

Chapter 5   Safety When Out

Purpose: To allow students to think of strategies for dealing
                with potentially dangerous situations
Time: 45 minutes
Materials: Paper, copies of 'what if' questions below, chalk-
                board or flipchart

Start by asking the students what their concerns are for their own
safety. Have them work in groups to come up with a list, which you
can then write on the board without comment.

Ask them how many of them have ever experienced an attack or
been mugged or threatened. The results of this are often surprising. In
one group of 110 fourteen-year-olds, 31 had been physically attacked
or mugged. Twenty-nine had never told their parents and the majority
were boys. They did not tell their parents for fear that the parents
would not let them out again.

If there is time, have the students make up a questionnaire for the
rest of the student body to see the extent of their experiences. We are
talking about stranger or acquaintance attacks here.

Have the students break into groups to discuss the 'what if' situations listed below. Ask each group to present three or four ideas to the
rest of the class. Students can also roleplay the situations.

If the students are reluctant to admit that they are at risk, ask them to
say what advice they would give to a younger child, such as a brother
or sister. (Be prepared for wisecracks!)

What if . . .

1. You are walking down the street alone and you think you are being
    followed?
    (a) It is daytime and you can see people in the distance.
    (b) It is late at night and no one is around.

2. You are approached by someone demanding money.
    (a) on a busy high street?
    (b) in a lonely back street?
    (c) and the person has a knife or another weapon?

3.   Someone actually grabs you and tries to pull you into a car or towards deserted grounds?

4.   You are home alone and a delivery person comes to the door with flowers, groceries, a package, etc., but you are not expecting anyone?

5.   A man comes to the door saying his car has broken down and his wife is having a baby, so can he phone for an ambulance?

6.   You are travelling on a bus/train/underground alone and:
      (a) someone flashes at you?
      (b) someone starts touching you?
      (c) someone whispers obscenities at you?
      (d) someone seems to be following you when you leave?
      (e) someone starts hitting you?

7.   You need to make an emergency telephone call, but you have no money?

8.   You are at a party. There are no adults in the house/flat. A gang of kids gate-crashes the party. The boy giving the party has not told his parents about the party and begs you not to call the police or his parents will kill him.

9.   You are jogging in the park with your Walkman on, and someone pulls you to the ground and starts attacking you?

10.   You miss the last bus home after a party?

11.   You come into your block of flats and a person you have never seen before comes up behind you and waits for you to open the door?

12.   You are getting into the lift alone and someone you vaguely know gets in, but makes you feel very uncomfortable?

13.   You are babysitting and the person who is supposed to take you home is drunk?

14.   You are in a public toilet and the person next to you tries to touch you?

15.   You come home alone and hear or see what appears to be a burglary going on in your flat/house?

Follow-up activities

Divide the students into groups again and ask them to devise a 'what if' questionnaire for the rest of the class/school. Have them administer the questionnaire and publish the results.

Chapter 6 Bullying

Purpose: To think of ways to deal with and eradicate bullying
Time: 45–60 minutes
Materials: List of questions, paper

Bullying has been a problem for many people, both the victims and the bullies. I would like to find out what you think about the problem and how you think it can be solved. If it is not a problem for you or anyone you know, perhaps you can think of what can be done either for younger children or for other people.

Divide the class into small groups, if possible, or have a large class discussion. Some of the issues and concerns can be raised with the following questions.

- Can you define bullying?
- What do you think are the characteristics of bullies?
- Why do people bully?
- Is it ever right to bully someone?
- What should people do if they know someone is being bullied?
- What if you see someone being bullied?
- Does anyone deserve to be bullied?
- Is there a problem with bullying in this school/neighbourhood/youth centre/institution, etc.?
- If so, what can be done about it?

This kind of work will start students talking about and recognising the problem. Their ideas and suggestions can be presented to the class (from small groups) or written up from the class discussion.

6a. Bullying Questionnaire

Purpose:	To devise a questionnaire to discover the extent of bullying
Time:	45 minutes to several sessions if the questionnaire is used with the school or institution
Materials:	Paper

Ask the students to devise a simple questionnaire, such as following.

Questionnaire about bullying

1. Have you ever been bullied?

   _____yes   _____no

2. At what age?

   _____under 5 _____5-11_____11-14 _____Over 14

3. Did/do you consider the bullying to have been

   _____no problem _____worrying _____frightening

   _____so bad that you didn't want to go out or to school

4. Did the bullying

   _____have no effect   _____some bad effect

   _____terrible effect   _____make you change your life in some way
   (e.g. change schools)

5. Is the bullying still happening?

   _____yes   _____no

6. If the bullying is still happening, where is it occurring?

   _____classroom   _____during sports   _____toilets

   _____after school   _____lunchroom   _____halls

   _____library   _____activities   _____everywhere

7. How often is it happening?

_____very seldom

_____once a month

_____once a week

_____once a day

_____several times a day

8. Is the bullying

    _____physical   _____verbal   _____racial

    _____sexual   _____emotional (being sent to coventry/ignored, etc.)

    _____threats   _____taking possessions/money

9. Do you know anyone who is being bullied, but has not told?

    _____yes   _____no

10. What do you think of bullies?

    _____no feeling   _____feel sorry for them   _____hate them

    _____like them

11. Who is responsible when bullying continues to go on?

    _____the bully _____the bully's parents _____the teachers

    _____the head_____the victim_____children who are not being bullied,

    but do not help the victim _____others

12. Please tick whether you are a _____girl _____boy

13. Was the bully (bullies)

    _____a girl   _____a boy   _____both

    _____a gang   _____teacher   _____member of staff

14. If you were or are being bullied, have you ever told anyone?

    _____yes   _____no

15. Did the bullying stop when you told?

    _____yes   _____no

16. Did the bullying become worse because you told?

    _____yes   _____no

17. Have you ever bullied anyone?   _____yes _____no

18. Are you bullying someone in this school now?
    _____yes _____no

19.   Will you now stop bullying?   _____yes   _____no

20.   What should be done about the problem of bullying?

. . . .

. . . .

. . . .

. . . .

. . . .

Once the questionnaire has been devised, it can be given to a class, form or the entire school. If done anonymously, it will probably give a fairly clear picture of:

- whether bullying is a problem
- where bullying is happening
- how many students are being bullied.

It may also give you practical suggestions from the students about how to combat the problem of bullying. Some suggestions from students and teachers which have worked include the following.

Suggestions that work

- Bully arbitration 'courts' or meetings run by students with help from staff – should be done as part of a whole school anti-bullying policy (see page 108)
- Meetings between bully and teacher/victim.
- Involving parents in meetings to address the problem and get their suggestions.
- Breaking the 'code of silence' that young people keep. Discuss making the school a 'telling school' in which it is the obligation of the students to tell – no 'bystanders' allowed.
- Having the students write roleplays about bullies and present them to the class or school.
- Having a poster contest with prizes for the best positive poster (art ability not necessary – the poster can be a slogan or pictures).
- Having students design a leaflet (example on page 106).
- Breaking up gangs of bullies (see page 104).
- Calling a school-wide assembly to discuss the problem of bullying.
- Working out a school anti-bullying policy, involving students and staff, and presenting the results to a school governors' or parents' meeting and to seek their support.
- Arranging for the bully to get counselling.
- Helping the victims become more assertive and self-confident. Discussing how to talk your way out of a fight and reinforcing the

message that your school does not support violence. Students could roleplay when it is wise to walk away from a situation:

> The bully is becoming physically abusive and is beginning to come towards you. What do you do?

- Having the students roleplay several situations and discuss them, deciding on which strategies might work. Is it wise to go on the offensive in some situations? Is it ever a good idea to just remain silent? Should you pour fuel on the fire by making the other person angrier?

- Asking the students if they think there would be situations when the police would be called if bullying was happening. This makes them think of some of the possible consequences to ongoing or violent bullying. Under what circumstances would the police be called – theft, extortion, physical attack? (See Lesson 13 'Common sense defence', for ways to get away from an attacker)

- Discussing the attitude of the students towards each other. Are they supportive? If someone is being bullied, do other students help, ignore or join in? What suggestions have the students for those who are not being bullied or those who are not the bullies?

- Asking the students to come up with a list of suggestions for staff to deal with bullying.

Suggestions for staff

The following is a list of suggestions for staff, compiled by a staff–student council meeting.

1. Tell the students from day one that bullying (verbal or physical) is *not* tolerated in the school. Everyone is expected to ensure that it does not happen and has the responsibility to tell – this is not telling tales.

2. In class, have the students discuss bullying: what it is, what can be done, etc.

3. Have the students do a school survey to find out what students, teachers and staff think about bullying. Is it a problem, should it go on, should children tell if they are being bullied?

4. Have the students compile the results of the survey and allow them to call a school assembly to announce the results.

5. Have a staff–student committee make up an anti-bullying policy and post it in the school. Give copies to parents or put it in the school handbook. An example of an anti-bullying school policy can be obtained from Kidscape by sending a large stamped addressed stamped envelope to Kidscape at the address in the 'Where to find help' section.

6.   Agree possible solutions (or punishments or consequences, if necessary) for bullying – these might include doing something constructive in the school such as cleaning graffiti off walls, helping younger children with reading or maths, apologising to the victim, replacing stolen or destroyed items, etc.

7.   Have the students discuss ways to help the bullies become part of the group.

8.   If bullying is going on, find out the facts, talk to the bullies and victims individually. If the bullying is about a particular issue (e.g. death, divorce, disfigurement), mount an education programme about the problem, but do not focus on a particular child. Call in parents, ask for their suggestions and solicit their support.

9.   If necessary break up the group dynamics by assigning places, keeping bullies at school at the end of the day, etc. Most bullying groups have a leader with other students being frightened of *not* bullying. Turn peer pressure against bullying and break up groups.

10.   Teach students to be assertive, using programmes such as Teenscape. Differences should be acceptable and never a cause for bullying. Reward and encourage children for individuality.

Breaking up bully gangs

It is difficult for teachers to deal with a gang of bullies. Anatol Pikas, a Swedish Professor of Psychology, suggests that the best way to deal with gang is to break them up from the very first meeting so that they cannot rely upon each other to keep up the gang mentality.

1.   Meet with victim or victims separately – have them write down what happened.

2.   Meet with each member of the gang separately – have them write down what happened.

3.   Agree with each member of the gang separately what you expect and discuss how he or she has broken the contract about guidelines for behaviour (see Lesson 6c, points 1–4).

4.   Meet with the gang as a group and have each member state what happened in your individual meeting; ensure that everyone is clear about what is expected.

5.   Prepare them to face their peer group – 'What are you going to say when you leave here?'

6.   Decide about involving the 'bully courts' – this will depend upon what you have agreed with the students.

7. Whatever is decided, reiterate to all students that they are all responsible if anyone is being bullied – there are no innocent bystanders.

8. Talk to the parents of all involved – show them the written statements.

9. Keep a file on bullying with all statements and penalties.

10. Teach victims strategies (as in Kidscape lessons).

11. Do not accept false excuses:
    — If it (the bullying) was an accident, did the children act by helping the victim or getting help or giving sympathy?
    — If it was just for a laugh, was everyone laughing?
    — If it was a game, was everyone enjoying it?

12. If a child is injured, take photographs of the injury.

13. If gangs of bullies from outside your school appear, take photographs – they tend to run when they see the camera.

14. If there is serious injury, contact the police.

6b. Bullying leaflet

Purpose:	To design a leaflet for students and parents about bullying
Time:	45–60 minutes or perhaps two sessions
Material:	Paper, copy of the sample leaflet

Ask the students to either design their own leaflet or use the following leaflet and modify it. A leaflet for teenagers and one for parents is available from Kidscape if you send a large stamped addressed envelope to Kidscape at the address in the 'Where to get help' section of this manual.

Sample Kidscape bullying leaflet

Bullying

Bullies make life miserable for many children. Some people are bullies because they are:

- Unhappy
- Insecure
- Bullied at home
- Not allowed to show feelings
- Cowards at heart
- Self hating

Bullies appear very powerful. They may even make it seem like the bullying is the victim's fault.

Help!

If bullying is chronic and severe, it is probably affecting many children. The behaviour must be stopped for the sake of the victims and the bullies.

Some things adults should do about bullying:

- Not allow it anywhere.
- Support children who are being bullied.

- Help the bullies to change their behaviour.
- Tell children to tell and back them up.
- Take bullying seriously and find out the facts when told about an incident of bullying.
- Inform parents if children are being bullied or if children are bullies at school.
- Meet with the bullies and the victims individually.
- Ensure that children, parents and teachers take responsibility for any bullying that goes on to anyone.
- Set up discussion groups and lessons about bullying.
- Break up groups of bullies by not allowing them to play, sit, eat (etc.) together.
- If bullying is happening on the way home, keep the bullies at school until everyone has left. Do not allow the bullies to leave together.
- Use peer pressure against bullying behaviour.
- Help students think about strategies to use.
- If necessary, help the children set up 'bullying courts' which decide how to deal with bullying. Roleplay situations.

Some things to do if you are being bullied

- Tell an adult you trust.
- Tell yourself that you don't deserve to be bullied.
- Get your friends together and say 'no' to the bully.
- Stay with groups of people, even if they are not your friends. There is safety in numbers.
- Try to ignore the bullying.
- Try not to show you are upset, which is difficult.
- If possible, avoid being alone in places where bullying happens.
- Try being assertive – shout 'No' loudly. Practise in front of a mirror.
- Walk quickly and confidently even if you don't feel that way inside. Practise!
- If you are in danger, get away. Do not fight to keep possessions.
- Fighting back may make it worse. If you decide to fight back, talk to an adult first.
- If you are different in some way, be proud of it! It is good to be an individual.

Contact

- The teacher, headteacher, parent governors on your school's board; the education welfare officer or the educational psychologist; your MP
- Citizen's Advice Bureaux [local directory]
- Children's Legal Centre
- ChildLine
- Samaritans [local directory]

6c. Student meetings of 'bully courts'

Purpose:	To involve students in helping to stop bullying
Time:	45 minutes
Material:	paper

'Bully courts' or student meetings are a useful way to get students to think about ways to stop bullying. Many schools use the 'bully court' as a drama roleplay rather than as an actual exercise. However, schools which have successfully used the 'bully courts' say that the involvement of students, as part of a whole-school anti-bullying policy, has positive effects because peer pressure works well in reducing bullying.

When setting up a student meeting of 'Bully court', consider the following suggestions that have worked for schools:

1. Agree guidelines for behaviour with students.

2. Sign individual contracts with each student regarding the guidelines.

3. Post the guidelines on bulletin boards throughout the school.

4. Call a school assembly and have students present the guidelines; include all staff, including playground supervisors.

5. As part of the guidelines, set up an arbitration court to rule on infractions.

6. The court could comprise four students, two elected by the student body and two appointed (as an honour) by the teachers.

7. One teacher would sit on the court (which could be called an Honour Court).

8. The term of office depends upon the agreement of the students – one school term would be suggested.

9. Unless there were an emergency, the court would meet once a week at a set time.

10. The court would be responsible for most infractions, unless they were serious enough to involve the police (i.e. assault) or there was a family problem which made it inappropriate.

11. Solutions and/or penalties would be written down and given to the

headteacher to be administered. There would be a right of appeal to the headteacher. Possible solutions and/or penalties should be in keeping with school policy – a list would be helpful.

12. The final 'verdict' of the court would be written down and filed, with copies going to all concerned parties.

13. School governors and parents would all receive information about the court and could be invited to a meeting to see a mock case and to discuss the issues.

14. The effectiveness of the court would be evaluated by students, parents and teachers.

6d. Keeping a 'bully' journal

Purpose: To help students empathise with victims and bullies
Time: 10 minutes a day for a week or more
Materials: Journal or paper

The following is a diary kept by a 14 year old boy to help him cope with the bullying that was happening. Use it as an example of keeping a journal, which can be fact or fiction or a mixture of both. The journal can be part of an English assignment and can be confidential between the teacher and student.
   A fact/fiction story by Nicholas Hargreaves

MY DIARY (the victim)

Tuesday 7th September

My first day back at school. I got pinned down in the playground and tortured. That's what it's like every day. Big boys in the seventh year look like giants to me. They prod and tickle me. I went to see the headmaster, Mr Clay, who just laughed and sent me to my lesson.

Wednesday 8th September

Prod! Poke! Thump! "Ouch!"

Thursday 9th September

Prod! Poke! Thump! "Ouch!"

Friday 10th September

Prod! Poke! thump! "Ouch!"

Wednesday 15th September

Every day's the same. I get bullied day in, day out. I can't help it, it's not my fault.
   Going on a nature trip today. Get away from those bullies. Mark, the only friend I've got, asked me how I got the black eye. "Fell off my bike." I said. It was too late to say anything now. I'd told a rotten sneaky lie and felt awful about it. But I hate to admit when someone asks me.

Friday 17th September

Day after day I'm feeling lonelier and lonelier. The only friend I've got is Mark, and of course, my parents. My other classmates seem to be on the bullies' side.

Monday 20th September

Oh, no! Conkering season! I can guess what that means. Boy, was I right. Conkers rained off my head. Seventh years again. It happens every year. Last year, I had lumps on my head for a week.

Friday 24th September

I'm feeling upset about the fact I've hardly got any friends, how people gang up on me and follow me. Why can't I lead a life like everyone else? What's so different about me?

   People having a knock-about with a football. I briefly approach them. They tell me to get lost. I now feel twice as bad at the thought of seeing Mark with them. I don't think he knows how much I feel for him. I don't think he'll ever know. I feel a great deal about my best friend, my only friend.

Tuesday 28th September

I went to see Mr Clay three times today. At last, he's starting to see my problem. I've finally got through to him. He knows what's wrong with me, especially now Mum is ringing him.

Friday 1st October

I think I will take up running as a hobby. I'll be able to get away from my enemies, run faster than them. Humph! There's Mr Clay watching me like a hawk, standing all alone in the middle of the playground with my hands in my pockets, feeling sorry for myself. He's been watching me since mum rang him on Tuesday. It's still no good he never seems to witness me getting bullied.

Monday 4th October

Tripped up in the playground today and banged my knee. That's all I had to do to make three seventh years come over and start laughing at me. One of them pushed me back over. They teased me just because I fell over. I looked across the playground. Was Mr Clay there? Of course not! Why should he be? After all, I'm only getting picked on by three giants.

Monday 11th October

It's almost a week before my birthday. Not that I'm going to get much. It's just something to look forward to.

I think Mr Clay must have something going for Mrs Evans. He's been hanging around with her and chatting to her for the last week. She's definitely been smiling to him when she sees him. That must be something, because she's usually an old grouch.

Thursday 14th October

I'm ashamed of Mark. He's told everyone about my birthday, especially the seventh years and I can now guess what's going to happen.

Friday 15th October

I've just had ten bumps to celebrate my birthday. Boy! Am I sore! Up, down; up, down; kicking my backside each time; banging it off the floor. Oh, no! Here they come with the eggs and flour.

Tuesday 19th October

Apart from the ordeal on Friday, I had a good birthday. Oh, dear! Here comes Mr Clay. He must have been told about Friday. Took me to his office and sat me down. "Ouch!"

Humph! He's lecturing on again about this, that and the other. I'm getting tired of this everyday. Why can't he just get round to the point?

Thursday 21st October

I still can't believe it. Mark is my true friend after all. It was him that told Mr Clay when I got the bumps, the egg and the flour. My best friend, Mark.

Friday 22nd October

We're breaking up for half-term. I'll get a rest from those awful seventh years. They'll probably gang up on me today so I shall stay in at dinner time and help clear up the tables. They ganged up on me before last summer. Took me a week to recover. A week off my holiday. But thank goodness last year's seventh years have left now.

Monday 1st November

Back to school again today after one very short week. Back with my best friend, Mark and my favourite teacher Mrs Giles. Today is a quiet day, a mild but wet day. Today's an ordinary day in which the birds sing and the wind whispers in the trees. Today's a very ordinary day in which I'm going to get bullied.

RICHARD'S DIARY (The Bully)

Tuesday 7th September

Back to school today. How boring. The only thing I missed in the holiday was beating up that weed, Nicholas. What a wimp! I only have to tap him and he goes to tell the headmaster, Mr Clay, after falling on the floor squawling like a baby.

Wednesday 8th September

Deep inside, I feel sorry for him. My mates and I go round every day and bully him when we pass him. Out comes Mr Clay and gives us a long lecture.

Friday 10th September

Prod! Poke! Slap! Thump! I can't help it; I laugh afterwards together with my mates while all the time I'm feeling depressed. My mum's in hospital. She's been suffering from kidney failure since January. The surgeons can't get more kidneys to replace her infected ones.

Monday 13th September

To make matters worse, my dad's been taking it out on me and beating me. That's probably the reason why I'm bullying Nicholas. I have been since mum went into hospital. He doesn't realise what a stressful time I've been through.

Tuesday 14th September

Oh, dear! Here he comes again.

I laid four on him; I couldn't stop myself. That's probably what my dad thinks when he's hit me.

Wednesday 15th September

Can't find him anywhere today. He must be off, sick. There's no one to take my depression out on. This is probably a good thing. One of these days, I might hurt him seriously then I would be in trouble. The problem is, I'm getting pleasure out of it, especially when I'm with my mates: John; Peter; John's best mate; Paul, my best mate; and Robert.

Friday 17th September

There he is, walking alone with his hands in his pockets.

Why didn't I leave him alone? My mates and I gathered in single file and followed him. He realised what was happening, turned round and shouted "PUSH OFF!" Instead of hitting him, we fell about laughing.

Monday 20th September

Conkering season starts today. Poor Nick! Out came the conkers and rapped him on the head. In he ran, dazed; crying. Out came Mr Clay, ranting and raving.

Thursday 23rd September

That Mark must be as big a wimp as Nicholas hanging around with hi
at times. There they are now. It's strange, the fact we bully Nicholas ar
not Mark. It's probably because Mark's not as soft.

Mark's just walked away; Nick's a loner once more and there are n
mates starting to gather round him.

Tuesday 28th September

My mates have just kicked a football at him. He turned round and it
him right in the mouth. He's gone in now, he went in with a bleeding li
Oh, no! Out comes Mr Clay yet again! It's the third time today.

He made me stand, facing the wall with my hands on my head. Wi
me? My mates have got away with it yet again.

Tuesday 5th October

I'm getting more depressed every day. My father's putting pressure c
me and I'm taking it all out on Nick. He was running towards the scho
this morning and I tripped him up. He fell down and cut his arm severel
At the time it happened, I laughed, but now I feel awful at the thought
it. People must think I'm nasty but it's not my fault. I just can't he
myself.

Friday 8th October

There he goes again, limping towards Mr Clay and holding his leg. M
mates have just given him more stick. It's all right for them. They get th
pleasure out of it while I just take everything out on him because I fe
hurt.

Thursday 14th October

Mark has just told us that it's Nick's birthday on Saturday – we had
force it out of him, though. We'll have to celebrate tomorrow instea
bring the eggs and flour, give him the kicks and do other things like tha

Friday 15th October

We've just given him ten bumps and pelted him with the eggs and flou
He's now running off home. My mates are still following him, throwi
eggs. I've just recovered from laughing, watching them run in the di
tance with Nick covered in gunge. It's the first time I've laughed like th
in ages.

Monday 18th October

Mark's just gone to tell Mr Clay. What a sneak. It must be about Frida
Wait till I get my hands on him. Crumbs! Out comes Mark now, tuggi

Mr Clay by the hand. Time to hide. He's just caught John and now he's after Paul.

Friday 22nd October

We're breaking up today for half-term and I can't find Nicholas anywhere. I feel so mad. My dad strapped me this morning for not cleaning my teeth. I just want to take it out on him; clear it from my system. He's nowhere to be seen. I want to make the most of bullying him anyway because I won't see him for a week.

Monday 1st November

Well, it's back to the old school again. What a life. From today onwards, I'm going to cut down bullying Nicholas. When I'm mad now, I'll just count to ten and take my problems out on Mr Clay. He'll understand. He will know why I've been bullying Nick.

Friday 5th November

I didn't tell him until today but he understood and forgave me. I'm a lot happier now. My dad's being looked after by a special hospital and I've gone to a children's home for a few weeks until my dad gets better.

Mr Clay is treating me to the bonfire and party tonight. From today onwards, I start a new life.

Chapter 7   Crime

Purpose:	To help students realise the effects of crime and to examine their own attitudes towards crime
Time:	45–60 minutes
Materials:	A copy of the list below for each student

You can begin the lesson by saying to the students something like:

Crime is something which affects us all. We are going to be discussing the problem of crime and how it affects you and others in the community.

Have the students divide into groups of six with the task of defining what they think crime is. The following exercise may help them to get started:

Using the list, you are to agree which of the crimes you would label

- *Extremely serious*
- *Serious*
- *Not serious.*

You must all agree to the label you put next to the crime. You cannot put for example, 'Serious/Not serious'. It must be one label only.

	Extremely Serious	Serious	Not Serious
Murder of an old lady	_____	_____	_____
Murder of an old man	_____	_____	_____
Murder of a child	_____	_____	_____
Murder of someone your age	_____	_____	_____
Murder of someone you love	_____	_____	_____
Rape of an old lady	_____	_____	_____
Rape of an old man	_____	_____	_____
Rape of a child	_____	_____	_____
Rape of someone your age	_____	_____	_____
Mugging of an old person	_____	_____	_____

Mugging of a young woman   _____   _____   _____

Mugging with a weapon   _____   _____   _____

Beating up an old person   _____   _____   _____

Beating up someone you love   _____   _____   _____

Beating up a person for
racial reasons   _____   _____   _____

Having a bicycle stolen   _____   _____   _____

An old person's pension
being stolen   _____   _____   _____

A mother stealing food
from a shop to feed her
children   _____   _____   _____

Shoplifting from a big
department store   _____   _____   _____

Shoplifting from a small
local shop   _____   _____   _____

A stranger stealing
something from a shop   _____   _____   _____

A friend stealing
something from a shop   _____   _____   _____

Getting drunk and smashing
a window   _____   _____   _____

Getting drunk and beating
someone up   _____   _____   _____

Making obscene comments
to a stranger on the street   _____   _____   _____

Someone making an obscene
telephone call to your home   _____   _____   _____

Flashing at a child   _____   _____   _____

Flashing at a person
your age   _____   _____   _____

Dropping a rock from a
bridge on to a motorway
or railway   _____   _____   _____

Stealing a car that belongs
to a poor person   _____   _____   _____

Stealing a car that belongs to a wealthy person	_____	_____	_____
'Joy riding'	_____	_____	_____
'Joy riding' causing injury	_____	_____	_____
Running down a pedestrian and driving off	_____	_____	_____
Under-age drinking	_____	_____	_____
Drinking and driving	_____	_____	_____
Sniffing glue/other solvents	_____	_____	_____
Using marijuana	_____	_____	_____
Using crack	_____	_____	_____
Using cocaine	_____	_____	_____
Using heroin	_____	_____	_____
Selling drugs	_____	_____	_____

After they have completed this exercise, ask the students to decide what punishment they would give to the perpetrator of the crimes on the list. You may give them suggestions, such as prison, community service, capital punishment, etc. They will not be bound by the law as it stands, but they are to be the judge/jury in making the decision.

Follow-up

- The list (and/or the questionnaire suggested below) will give you a basis from which to invite the Crime Prevention Officer, if appropriate, to explain to the class about the various categories of crimes and what usually happens to those who are arrested.
- Have the students discuss how they are affected by crime and ask them to share any experiences they may have had as victims of crime
- Ask the students to devise and use a questionnaire with students, teachers and parents to find out their attitudes towards crime and how many of them have been victims. Have them publish the results and use it as a talking point about what can be done.

Perhaps the findings will indicate that theft is a problem in school Have the students devise a plan to try to stop the problem.

To follow up, the students may want to write to newspapers with their concerns or approach local radio stations about having a panel of young people present their views.

Decide if you want to invite speakers to come in to discuss crime, the law or other issues which arise during discussion.

This lesson may bring up strong feelings and engender disagreements about the issue of crime and how the law is/is not enforced. It is important that the students have a chance to air their views and discuss their feelings.

Chapter 8   Rights and Responsibilities

Purpose: To enable students to understand that, although w
all have rights, there are responsibilities which g
along with those rights
Time: 45 minutes
Materials: Copy of the list and questions below, paper, chal
board or flipchart

You may wish to begin the lesson with a statement about rights or as
the students to name some of their rights:

*We all have certain rights, such as the right to breathe and the right to ea
Can you name some of your rights?*

Write the students suggestions on the board. Taking this as a basi
have the students divide into groups with the task of putting thes
rights into three categories – on which they must agree.
These categories could be:

- Essential rights for everyone
- Good rights to have, but not essential
- Luxury rights

Or you could come up with your own categories. Below is a suggeste
list which could be used to prime the discussion or to supplement th
students' list.

Rights

	Essential	Good	Luxury
Education	_____	_____	_____
Work	_____	_____	_____
Personal safety	_____	_____	_____
To vote	_____	_____	_____
Life	_____	_____	_____
Fair trial	_____	_____	_____

Money	_____	_____	_____
Food	_____	_____	_____
Job	_____	_____	_____
Holidays	_____	_____	_____
CD player	_____	_____	_____
Decent clothes	_____	_____	_____
To go out with friends	_____	_____	_____
To say no to unwanted touching	_____	_____	_____
Television set	_____	_____	_____
Home	_____	_____	_____
To have children	_____	_____	_____
To have medical care	_____	_____	_____
To take drugs	_____	_____	_____
To be free from racial attacks	_____	_____	_____
To drink alcohol	_____	_____	_____

Alternatively, have the students in small groups come up with a list of rights for each category, including the ones you have written on the board.

When the students have listed the rights in categories, ask them to discuss how they feel about their rights.

- Do they think that putting rights into categories works?
- What rights do they have?
- Which of those listed do they consider most essential for themselves? Their families? Their friends?
- What would they do if their rights were taken away?
- Are there countries and cultures which have a different view of people's rights? What do they think of these views?

esponsibilities

- If we have rights, are there responsibilities that go with the rights? For example, if we have the right to personal safety, what are our responsibilities if:
  (a) we see a stranger, a friend or someone in our family being bullied?
  (b) we see a stranger, a friend or someone in our family being racially or sexually harassed?

(c) we see a stranger, a friend or someone in our family being robbed

(d) we see a stranger, a friend or someone in our family being attacked?

(e) we know someone who is homeless?

(f) we know someone who is being beaten regularly?

(g) we know that children are being starved or mistreated?

(h) we know someone who caused injury by 'joy riding', but hasn been caught?

- Do we have a responsibility to do something if we see or know abou

(a) a stranger (friend, family) sniffing glue?

(b) a stranger (friend, family) smashing a shop front window?

(c) a stranger (friend, family) littering the pavement?

(d) a stranger (friend, family) creating a disturbance at a footba match?

Have the students think of other situations that might raise the issue o responsibility such as:

- Under-age drinking
- Drinking/driving
- Having an elderly neighbour or relative who needs assistance
- Having a baby
- Aerosol cans and the environment
- Seeing a child fall into a river
- Having to take care of an infirm parent or relative
- Having a sibling/friend with an illness or who has special neec because of something such as being paralysed, blind, hearin impaired

There are numerous examples that the students can bring up.

When the students have discussed the issues about responsibilitie ask them to either make up a roleplay around one of the situations o their choice showing how they might deal with the it, or write a stor or draw a picture.

Follow-up

- The lesson could be the basis for follow-up activities such as cuttin stories from the newspaper or relating stories from the televisio about rights and/or responsibilities.
- Students could have discussions about responsibility in relationship crime, bullying, abuse, gambling, addiction, etc.
- For the school community, perhaps a project on the rights an responsibilities of the students and staff to each other and th surrounding community would be appropriate. For example, if ther is a problem with shoplifting from a local shop, what are th responsibilities of the students and/or staff? What about the sho

keeper? If there are a group of students bothering other students, what could be done?

You may want to come back to these issues as problems or queries arise throughout the year.

Chapter 9   Relationships

Purpose: To help students understand about their responsi-
               bilities and rights in relationships with others
Time: 40–60 minutes
Materials: Questionnaires, paper

The first part of this lesson is appropriate for all teenagers. In the
second part, you will need to decide which of the two questionnaires
below best suits your students.

   If you have a mixed school, separate the boys and girls. Ask that
each group list:

- What qualities they look for in a friend of the same sex.
- What qualities they look for in a friend of the opposite sex.
- What qualities they look for in a date.
- What qualities they would expect from all of the above.

When the class is together, discuss the similarities and differences. The
'qualities' sometimes expected for a date include physical attractive-
ness or material goods. Discuss why the lists are different or the same.
Ask the boys to make comments about the girls' lists and vice versa.

   Have the students break into small mixed groups to produce one list
of qualities they would expect in anyone – male, female or a date. As
this usually engenders much discussion, allow the groups plenty of
time.

   Give the students the questionnaire that follows in this section.
Please note the age differences and give the appropriate questionnaire
to your class. It may take 10–15 minutes for them to complete it.

   Do not collect the questionnaire, but use it as the basis for discussion. Suggested answers are given, but as it says, these are only to be
used as a guide.

Questionnaire for young teenagers

(from *Keeping safe, a practical guide to talking with children*, Michele
Elliott, Hodder Headline 1994)

This questionnaire is designed to be used as a tool for communicating
with young people about keeping safe from assault. It is not meant to

be a test that is marked, but a way of opening up the subject without being alarmist. You may not always agree with the answers; some could be true or false depending upon the circumstances. The answers are given as a guide.

The questionnaire does not mention sex abuse or rape, but does use the word assault. It can be used with younger or less mature teens. The other questionnaire on the following pages is for older teens.

Questions

1.	You have the right to be safe.	T	F
2.	You should always keep secrets if you promise not to tell	T	F
3.	A bribe is given to make you do something you do not want to do.	T	F
4.	People are either good or bad.	T	F
5.	Only bad people who look strange hurt children.	T	F
6.	Adults do not always believe children.	T	F
7.	Children should always obey adults.	T	F
8.	You sometimes have the right to break rules.	T	F
9.	It is a good idea to answer the telephone by repeating your name or your telephone number.	T	F
10.	You should never lie.	T	F
11.	You should never fight back if someone attacks you.	T	F
12.	You have the right to tell anyone, even someone you know and trust, not to touch you in any way that makes you feel uncomfortable.	T	F
13.	Jealousy is a sign of true love.	T	F
14.	You should never hurt anyone's feelings.	T	F
15.	Looking foolish in front of others is really embarrassing.	T	F
16.	Boys and girls are encouraged to be sensitive and gentle with each other.	T	F
17.	When a child is assaulted, the offender is usually a stranger.	T	F
18.	Girls are assaulted much more often than boys.	T	F
19.	The vast majority assaults are committed by men.	T	F
20.	The best way to escape a potential assault is to vomit.	T	F
21.	A 'real man' shows the girl that he is the boss.	T	F

22. Generally the more attractive a boy or girl is the greater the chance of being assaulted.   T   F

23. It is sometimes the victim's fault that he or she was assaulted.   T   F

24. People are much safer from assault at home.   T   F

25. If you or someone you know is assaulted, you should tell a trusted adult immediately.   T   F

Suggested answers

1. **You have the right to be safe.**   True

2. **You should always keep secrets if you promise not to tell**.   False
Some secrets should not be kept. If anyone asks you to keep touching a secret or if you feel confused, uncomfortable or frightened by a secret, find a trusted adult to tell.

3. **A bribe is given to make you do something you do not want to do.**   True

4. **People are either good or bad.**   False

5. **Only bad people who look strange hurt children.**   False

6. **Adults do not always believe children**.   True
If the person you tell a problem to does not believe you, keep telling until someone does.

7. **Children should always obey adults**.   False
In order to keep safe, it may be necessary to disobey an adult.

8. **You sometimes have the right to break rules.**   True
To keep safe, it may be necessary to disobey an adult.

9. **It is a good idea to answer the telephone by repeating your name or your telephone number**   False

10. **You should never lie**.   False
You may need to lie to stay safe.

11. **You should never fight back if someone attacks you.**   False
If you feel in danger, you should do whatever you can to keep safe, such as kick, yell, bite, etc.

12. **You have the right to tell anyone, even someone you know and trust, not to touch you in any way that makes you feel uncomfortable.**   True
You have the right to say who touches your body.

13. **Jealousy is a sigh of true love.** False
Love depends upon mutual trust. Jealousy is based
upon lack of trust.

14. **You should never hurt anyone's feelings.** False
In order to keep yourself safe, you may have to say 'no'
to someone you know and like, which might hurt his
or her feelings.

15. **Looking foolish in front of others is really
embarrassing.** True
But do not be afraid to look foolish if you feel inside that
something is wrong. If you think you should leave
a party, for example, because you do not like what is
happening, do leave even if you are embarrassed. It
might keep you safe.

16. **Boys and girls are encouraged to be sensitive and
gentle with each other.** False
Girls and boys should make it clear that they like each
other are to be kind. Some boys think that girls only like
the 'macho' type.

17. **When a child is assaulted, the offender is usually
a stranger.** False
Over 75% of people who assault children are known to
the children.

18. **Girls are assaulted much more often than boys.** False
Boys are almost as much at risk as girls, though boys
less often report an assault.

19. **The vast majority of assaults are committed by men.** True
Over 90% of reported assaults are committed by men.
However, most men would never attack anyone and some
women do assault children.

20. **The best way to escape a potential assault is to vomit.** False
Although it may work, conversations with offenders
indicate that these kinds of tactics make them angry,
rather than disgusted. Many people feel than an
immediate spirited physical self-defence, including loud
yelling, kicking, hitting, etc, is best because the element
of surprise helps the victim to get away. Some people
have successfully talked their way out of dangerous
situations. Each person must decide what is best
according to the circumstances.

21. **A 'real man' shows the girl that he is the boss.** False
Why should one partner be boss?

22. **Generally the more attractive a girl or boy is the greater the chance of being assaulted**.   False
Studies have shown that being physically attractive has nothing to do with assault.

23. **It is sometimes the victim's fault that he or she was assaulted**.   False
It is always the offender's fault. No one deserves to be assaulted.

24. **People are much safer from assault at home**.   False
Several surveys have shown that many assaults happened in either the victim's or the assailant's home.

25. **If you or someone you know is assaulted, you should tell a trusted adult immediately**.   True
Think about people who would believe you and who would help you make a decision about what to do. An assault is too big a burden to carry in secret and getting help early will often lessen the trauma.

Questionnaire for older teenagers

One way to begin talking with young people about keeping safe from sexual abuse and assault is to give them this questionnaire or take it with them. It is not meant to be a quiz to be marked, but a basis for communication. Although answers are given, in some cases you may disagree with them. The desired outcome should be that teenagers think about and plan what to do if they are placed in a dangerous situation. This isn't a contest to get the 'right' answer.

This questionnaire does mention the terms 'sex abuse' and 'rape' and should be used with more mature teenagers.

Questions

1. You have the right to tell anyone, even someone you know and trust, not to touch you in any way that makes you feel uncomfortable.   T   F

2. When a girl says 'no' to a boy, she frequently means 'yes'   T   F

3. A boy or girl has a right to expect more than a kiss after he or she has spent money on a date.   T   F

4. Jealousy is a sign of true love.   T   F

5. Birth control is the female's responsibility.   T   F

6. Boys and girls are encouraged to be sensitive and gentle with each other.   T   F

7. Sexual frustration can be physically harmful.   T   F

8. People who fantasise about being seduced have
    emotional problems.   T   F

9. Most date rapes occur because the assailants have been
    teased to the point that they cannot control themselves.   T   F

10. Alcohol and/or drugs can lower inhibitions about
    engaging in sexual activity.   T   F

11. When a child is molested, the molester is usually
    a stranger.   T   F

12. Girls are molested much more often than boys.   T   F

13. The vast majority of sexual abusers are men.   T   F

14. The best way to escape a potential rapist is to vomit.   T   F

15. A 'real man' shows the girl that he is the boss.   T   F

16. Generally the more attractive a girl or boy is, the higher
    the chance of being sexually assaulted.   T   F

17. When a person is sexually assaulted, he or she usually
    has done something to provoke it.   T   F

18. It is against the law for a boy to engage in sexual
    intercourse with a girl under 16, even with her consent.   T   F

19. Sexual gratification is the major reason for rape.   T   F

20. Males who are sexually assaulted suffer the same kind
    of emotional trauma as female victims.   T   F

21. People are much safer from sexual assault at home.   T   F

22. Fewer than half of all rapes are reported to the police.   T   F

23. An assailant rarely finds it necessary to use a weapon
    to commit rape.   T   F

24. People who sexually assault others are psychologically
    disturbed.   T   F

25. Rapists are secret, solitary offenders who usually attack
    their victims when the rapist is alone.   T   F

26. Teenage and adult victims of sexual assault seldom know
    the identity of the offender.   T   F

27. Sexual assault is usually an unplanned, spontaneous act.   T   F

28. There are many false reports of rape by women seeking
    revenge on their boyfriends.   T   F

29. If a female victim feels uncomfortable talking with a male police officer, she has the right to request that a female officer be called.   T   F

30. As the rape victim is often unprotected by contraceptives, she will probably become pregnant.   T   F

31. The victim is allowed to have a friend stay with her or him during the medical examination or questioning   T   F

32. During an investigation of a rape, the victim can refuse to answer questions irrelevant to the rape.   T   F

33. If a person is raped, her or his name will be published by the media reporting her case.   T   F

34. As a rule, the victim of sexual assault can be asked questions in court about her or his sexual conduct.   T   F

35. Gay teenagers are never sexually assaulted.   T   F

36. If you or someone you know has been sexually assaulted, you should tell a trusted adult immediately.   T   F

Suggested answers

1. **You have the right to tell anyone, even someone you know and trust, not to touch you in any way that makes you feel uncomfortable**.   True
   As a high percentage of the assaults on teenagers are by an adult known to them, it is important to learn to say 'no' not only to strangers but also to friends, family members or acquaintances.

2. **When a girl says 'no' to a boy, she frequently means 'yes'**.   False
   This attitude is left over from old films and books. Boys and girls should discuss together their ideas about mixed messages so that both understand the expectations and the misconceptions of the other.

3. **A boy or girl has a right to expect more than a kiss after he or she has spent money on a date**.   False
   If this is his or her attitude, pay your own way.

4. **Jealousy is a sign of true love**.   False
   Love depends upon mutual trust. Jealousy is based upon lack of trust.

5. **Birth control is the female's responsibility**.   False
   It should be a shared responsibility.

6. **Boys and girls are encouraged to be sensitive and gentle with each other**. False

Some boys believe that being tough and macho is what girls expect of them. This should be discussed so that girls and boys can decide what they value in a relationship.

7. **Sexual frustration can be physically harmful**. False

No way! Still, you might hear it as an excuse from someone who is pressuring you into having sex, so be prepared to say NO.

8. **People who fantasise about being seduced have emotional problems**. False

Some people have 'seduction' fantasies. In the fantasy, they are in control; they choose the 'assailant', place, circumstances, etc. The reality of sexual assault is different – violent and sadistic.

9. **Most date rapes occur because the assailants have been teased to the point that they cannot control themselves**. False

This attitude blames the victim. Sexual assault occurs because the assailant has problems with anger, self-control, aggression, hostility and power.

10. **Alcohol and/or drugs can lower inhibitions about engaging in sexual activity**. True

Studies have shown this to be true for both sexes.

11. **When a child is molested, the molester is usually a stranger**. False

The child knows the attacker in at least 75% of the reported cases of child molestation.

12. **Girls are molested much more often than boys**. False

Statistics vary, but boys are almost as much at risk as girls. The victimisation of boys is reported less often, partly because of the fear of being branded as a homosexual after an attack.

13. **The vast majority of sexual abusers are men**. True

Over 90% of reported attacks were committed by men, but some women do sexually abuse children and young people.

14. **The best way to escape a potential rapist is to vomit**. False

Although it may work, conversations with convicted rapists indicate that these kinds of tactics make them angry, rather than disgusted. Many people feel that an immediate spirited physical defence, including loud yelling, kicking, hitting, etc is best because the element of surprise would help the victim to get away. Some people have successfully talked their way out of rape, but each person must decide what to do according to the circumstances.

15. **A 'real man' shows the girl that he is the boss.**   False
Why should one partner be the boss? This implies that the girl is incapable of directing her own life. It places her in the same category as a docile pet.

16. **Generally the more attractive a girl or boy is, the higher the chance of being sexually assaulted.**   False
Studies of assault victims have shown that being physically attractive has nothing to do with sexual assault.

17. **When a person is sexually assaulted, he or she usually has done something to provoke it.**   False
In the USA, the National Commission on the Causes and Prevention of Violence did a study on crimes of violence and paid particular attention to the role of the victim in the cases of murder, assault, robbery and rape. The commission wanted to determine whether victims of these crimes in any way provoked them or rashly touched off the action against them. It was discovered that victims of sexual assault were responsible for less provocative behaviour or unwitting collusion than victims of murder, assault or robbery. The cases on file of the rape or sexual assault of individuals of all ages, from 3-month-old babies to 97-year-old women and men, show how ridiculous this myth is.

18. **It is against the law for a boy to engage in sexual intercourse with a girl under sixteen, even with her consent.**   True
The legal age of consent is sixteen.

19. **Sexual gratification is the major reason for rape.**   False
Rape is about violence, not sex. If you hit someone over the head with your rolling pin, it is not called cooking.

20. **Males who are sexually assaulted suffer the same kind of emotional trauma as female victims.**   True
Sexual assaults on males are reported even less than assault on females and there is no national support system such as the Rape Crisis Centres for male victims. However, there are some local projects and some Rape Crisis Centres will now talk with men and boys and refer them to local helplines or centres. Victim Support has a list of numbers. (See the 'Where to get help' section at the end of this book.)

21. **People are much safer from sexual assault at home.** False
In several surveys, it was found that many sexual assaults happened either in the victim's or the assailant's home.

22. **Fewer than half of all rapes are reported to the police.** True
Only one in twelve is reported, according to a London survey.

23. **An assailant rarely finds it necessary to use a weapon to commit rape.** True
Only a small proportion of sexual assaults involve weapons. Most assailants use superior size and fear to subdue victims.

24. **People who sexually assault others are psychologically disturbed.** False
Most test as 'normal' on psychological tests.

25. **Rapists are secret, solitary offenders who usually attack their victims when the rapist is alone.** True
In a London survey of women conducted by Ruth Hall in 1985 (*Ask any woman*, Falling Wall Press 1985), it was found that only in one in one hundred cases involved more than one assailant.

26. **Teenage and adult victims seldom know the identity of the rapist.** False
In the survey mentioned in question 25, over 60% of the attackers were known to the victim.

27. **Sexual assault is usually an unplanned, spontaneous act.** False
Most sexual assaults are planned.

28. **There are many false reports of rape by women seeking revenge on their boyfriends.** False
In a study in New York of all the reported rapes in one year, only 2% turned out to be false.

29. **If a female victim feels uncomfortable talking with a male police officer, she has the right to request that a female officer be called.** True
Although a victim has the right to request this, the police have no obligation to provide a female officer. The police do try to comply with this request, if at all possible.

30. **As the rape victim is often unprotected by contraceptives, she will probably become pregnant.** False
Only a small percentage of rape victims become pregnant.

31. **The victim is allowed to have a friend stay with her or him during the medical examination or questioning.**   True
This can be a family member or close friend.

32. **During an investigation of a rape, the victim can refuse to answer questions irrelevant to the rape.**   True
Questions about a victim's personal life, not relevant to the rape, need not be answered.

33. **If a person is raped, her or his name will be published by the media reporting the case.**   False
Rape victims are entitled to anonymity before, during and after the trial.

34. **As a rule, the victim of sexual assault can be asked questions in court about her or his sexual conduct.**   False
In court a victim may not be asked questions about previous sexual conduct unless the judge is satisfied that these questions are relevant to the defence.

35. **Gay teenagers are never sexually assaulted.**   False
Gay teenagers often do not report sexual assaults, but they can be victims and need to report what happened and seek help.

36. **If you or someone you know has been sexually assaulted, you should tell a trusted adult immediately.**   True
Think about the people who would believe you and who would help you in making a decision about what to do. Sexual assault is too big a burden to carry in secret and getting supportive help early will often lessen the trauma. If you feel completely alone, telephone your local Samaritans or Rape Crisis Centre for information – the numbers are in your local directory. Also ring ChildLine – it is a 24-hour telephone service for cchildren or teenagers in distress.

Chapter 10 Abuse

Purpose:	To better understand child abuse
Time:	60 minutes
Materials:	Paper, news reports of child abuse

Ask the students to divide into groups and spend ten minutes defining what they consider to be abuse. Many of them will have heard the terms physical and sexual abuse from the television or radio or from discussions with family and friends. Having the students define abuse avoids the problem of giving them too much information (in case of younger students, particularly).

Take their definitions and compile a list of their ideas. You will probably find that they include:

- Beating
- Biting
- Burning
- Hitting
- Rape
- Sexual abuse
- Starvation

With younger students, you may not wish to use the terms 'rape' and 'sexual abuse' unless they do. You will probably find that they know the terms, but parents may object if you *introduce* concepts that they feel their teenagers are not ready to understand.

Ask the students to define the various forms of abuse (listed below). Ask groups to find definitions from books, newspaper articles, television programmes, etc.

If the students ask you for your definition of abuse, you can use your own or the following.

Physical abuse:
Physical abuse implies physically harmful action directed against a child; it is usually defined by an inflicted injury such as bruises, burns, head injuries, fractures, abdominal injuries, or poisoning. (C.H. Kempe)

Sexual abuse:
Sexual abuse is any exploitation of children under the age of 16 for the

sexual pleasure, gratification or profit of an adult or significantly older person. This ranges from obscene telephone calls, indecent exposure (flashing), taking pornographic pictures, attempted intercourse, rape or incest. (Michele Elliott)

Emotional abuse:

Emotional abuse includes a child being continually terrorised, berated or rejected. (C.H. Kempe)

Neglect:

Neglect can be a very insidious form of maltreatment, which can go on for a long time. It implies the failure of the parents to act properly in safeguarding the health, safety and well-being of the child. It includes nutritional neglect, failure to provide medical care or to protect a child from physical and social danger. (C.H. Kempe)

All these forms of abuse can be related. For example, a child who is physically abused is also emotionally abused. The students can discuss how abuse is interrelated.

Ask the students what their concerns are about the various forms of abuse. Does it make them sad, angry, confused when they hear about a young child being abused in some way?

- What do they think should be done to protect children?
- What are their views about the people who abuse children?
- What would they suggest to *help* an abuser who was their own age?

You could ask the students to write a report about a recent newspaper case of abuse, chosen by them. They could also do group work and come up with an oral report for the class about how their group feels and what they think should happen.

The students could set up a trial regarding a case of abuse and decide how they would change the laws or if they would leave them as they were with regard to abuse of children.

These exercises give the students a chance to express their feelings and concerns before going on to talk about protecting themselves from abuse. Try not to focus too heavily on just sexual abuse as it is important to discuss all forms of abuse.

Listed below are some cases of abuse which could be used as the basis of class discussion. It is better to have students bring in cases but the ones below are given as additional material.

Cases

These cases have all been reported in the media. The names and some of the details have been slightly altered to protect students in the unlikely event that the people concerned are familiar to someone in the local community.

Child murdered by foster father

A foster father accused of murdering a two-year-old boy was remanded in custody today. The man, G. Simmons, aged 31, is also accused of causing the boy's sister grievous bodily harm.

According to social services, both children had behavioural problems and had a tendency to inflict injuries on themselves. Their natural parents had abused the children.

Doctors said the boy had suffered severe non-accidental wounding, including haemorrhaging, indicating severe shaking, grip marks around his elbow and knee, and bruising of the jaw, consistent with being hit. There were also burn marks on the body from cigarettes.

The case has been adjourned until October.

Prison for scout master

A scout master was jailed for three months yesterday after admitting repeatedly indecently assaulting teenage boys after getting them drunk.

M Taylor, aged 46, a pillar of society and a respected member of his community, abused six boys between the ages of 13 and 16.

His crime was discovered after one of the boys told senior officials what had happened.

When passing sentence, the judge said that parents and children needed to be protected from this sort of abuse and that Mr Taylor was a danger to young boys.

Child locked cupboard

Police discovered a six-year-old girl chained by the ankle and locked in a three- by two-foot cupboard under the stairs. The child is suffering from malnutrition and appears unable to talk or walk properly. The girl has burns and sores over most of her body and has been admitted to hospital.

The girl's parents said the child was 'always a problem and never did what she was told'. They have been arrested.

A police officer said today that it was the worst case of child abuse he had seen in 20 years.

ollow-up

Themes in advertising

The students can use this exercise to debate and consider whether the use of children in the media could be contributing to the problem of child sexual abuse.

How do the images of children and young people in the media affect attitudes towards sexuality and sexual abuse?

What are the advertisers trying to achieve by portraying children and young people as sexual objects?

Have the students collect 'good' and 'bad' examples of images of children and young people used in advertising. These can come from television, newspapers, advertising boards and magazines. Ask them to analyse:

- What the advertiser is trying to sell
- What the overt messages are
- What the hidden messages are
- If they feel the image is 'healthy' not harmful
- If they feel that this image is harmful and could contribute to the problem of child sexual abuse and why
- If there is anything that can be done about the images that are deemed to be inappropriate

Have the students present their findings either in groups or individually. If they wish, have the class write a letter to an advertiser setting out their concerns.

This exercise can be used as a debate, a research project or a project that could be presented to other classes or to a group of teachers or parents. The students may wish to make a poster or mural using these images and ask other students or teachers for their opinions.

Chapter 11 Getting Help

Purpose:	To enable students to get help for themselves or others in case of bullying, abuse or other problems
Time:	60 minutes
Materials:	Telephone book, agony columns in magazines, leaflets

Ask the students to bring in any source which might list organisations that help with problems.
   Ask them:

> *Where would you turn if you were worried about a case of abuse, bullying, drug-taking or an alcohol problem or anorexia or gambling or AIDS?*

   Ask the students, working in groups, to try to come up with all the sources of help they can contact or find. You might assign each group an area or just let them cover all the possible problems – it depends upon the amount of time you have available.
   The section 'Where to get help' at the end of this manual can be used if necessary to supplement the list the students compile. However, it is best that the students do their own research as far as possible.
   Ask the students to brainstorm how they could use the information they have gathered. Suggestions might include making posters to put up around the school or community, or producing a leaflet for the students to use.
   Knowing where to turn if there is a problem is a useful basis for all the lessons. This lesson can be used on its own or as a follow-up to any chapter by just asking the students to research help for that particular topic.
   When the students have compiled their list, post it or give everyone a copy. If possible, it is best to give everyone a copy because it can be kept by anyone needing help who may be too frightened or shy to ask.

Chapter 12 Keeping Safe From Abuse

Purpose:	To help students realise that sexual abuse is mor likely to be perpetrated by a known person than by stranger
Time:	40–60 minutes
Materials:	Chalkboard or flipchart, paper

Note. When presenting this to younger teens, you may wish to avoi using the term 'sexual abuse' unless the parents have agreed. You wi most likely find that the students are not bothered and will use th terms freely but that parents are concerned. Follow whatever guide lines you have worked out with the parents and the school governor You could, for example, use the term 'abuse' or 'assault'.

Make sure that the students know where to turn for help – eithe teach Lesson 11 or give the students a copy of the 'Where to get hel section at the end of this manual before you teach Lesson 12. Yo may also wish to point out the people (perhaps including yoursel who are available to help, should anyone wish to talk privately.

The lesson can be started with a statement such as:

Talking about staying safe from abuse sometimes makes people nervou You might feel like laughing or telling jokes or just acting silly. Rememb that we need to be sensitive to one another when discussing these issue Some research has shown that as many as one in ten young people has a [sexually] abusive experience before reaching the age of 16. There may people in this class who have been abused and it is not funny to be abuse either physically or sexually or emotionally. First let's find out what yo know about the problem.

Write on the board:

WHO   WHERE   WHEN   WHY
(victims and abusers)

Ask the students to get into small groups and come up with a list who the abusers are, who the victims are, where abuse happens, whe it happens and why they think it happens. It can take a whole lesson you can put a time limit on it. It usually takes at least 20–30 minute
The students may tackle one form of abuse and you can repeat tl

exercise for other forms, or you may have them combine the various forms of abuse. It tends to work better if they do one at a time, but how you teach it will depend on the time you have and the ability and interest of the students.

When the students have compiled their lists, write their ideas on the board under the headings. Taking sexual abuse as an example, it may look something like:

WHO	WHERE/WHEN	WHY
ABUSERS		
Druggies	Dark	For kicks
Weirdos	Alleys	Hatred
Maniacs	Lifts	Power
Men	Parks	Can't help it
Strangers	Cars	Sex
Women	Deserted places	Crazy
Teachers	Home	Angry
Doctors	Friend's house	Evil
Parents	Assailant's house	Abused
Someone known	Cinemas	
Acquaintances		
Vicars		
VICTIMS		
Girls		
Women		
Prostitutes		
Children		
Boys		
Old ladies		
Men		

When everything is written on the board, go back and circle the most common factors:

- Most (75%) of the offenders are known to the victims.
- The *reported* offenders are mainly male (95%). Here emphasise that this does not mean that most men are abusers. Also although there are few reported cases of abuse by women, it does exist and is equally traumatic for the victim as abuse by a man.
- Although there are more reported girls as victims, many experts in the field believe that boys just do not report abuse.
- Most abuse or assaults take place in the home of the victim or in the home of the offender.
- Most offenders appear to be quite normal and come from every class, race, occupation and background – power and anger are often the motivating factor. Though many of the abusers were themselves abused, most abused children do not grow up to abuse others.

For physical abuse, the profile would probably emphasise parents, though being beaten up by a stranger would also be physical abuse.

Be certain to state that it is not always possible to say 'no' and get away and that sometimes people have no choice. This is in case a student in your class has already been abused so that he or she will not feel responsible for what happened. You can say something like:

> *'It is never your fault if you are abused, but there are some possible strategies which either could work avoid a difficult or dangerous situation or which might help if you find yourself in such a situation. Some of these we have discussed in previous lessons, others may be new ideas from you.*

Ask the students to brainstorm what they might do if someone tried to abuse/assault them or what they would do if it did happen (i.e. getting help).

Students may come up with ideas such as:

- Tell a friend [Suggest that the friend helps them to tell someone else like a school nurse or a parent or another trusted adult.]
- Kick the attacker [Perhaps, but make sure you can get away.]
- Yell
- Get away

Allow all suggestions, as some may help a student who needs to tell to decide what to do. We can only suggest to students what they may do. The ultimate choice to *tell* about abuse is with them. Otherwise, adults can only act upon symptoms and suspicions.

Chapter 13 Common Sense Defence

Purpose: To teach young people ways to physically protect
                 themselves
Time: 60 minutes
Materials: Large empty space, if possible

Make sure that you have parental agreement if you are going to teach
teenagers any form of physical self-defence.

Please note that in the lessons that follow the attackers are referred
to as both male and female. This is to ensure that the students are
aware that an attacker can be either male or female.

*The best form of self-defence is to get away from a dangerous situation as
quickly as possible and to avoid getting into dangerous situations. Can you
think of some common sense ideas for avoiding danger?*

Suggestions

- Avoid taking short-cuts through dark or deserted places.
- Never hitch-hike.
- If someone approaches you asking directions, keep your distance or
  walk away and pretend not to hear.
- If you are threatened, yell and run away, if possible.
- If you are being followed, go into a shop or towards people.
- Try crossing the road to see if the person follows.
- Do not wear a personal stereo as it prevents your being aware of what
  is happening around you.
- Avoid empty carriages on trains.
- On buses or the underground, sit near the driver or guard.

The students should come up with their own suggestions, but use the
following if necessary.

- If you are attacked, think of what you might do. Would you talk your
  way out of it or pretend to do what you are asked, while waiting for a
  chance to get away? Only you can decide what to do in the event.
- If you do have to defend yourself, take a deep breath and try not to
  panic. Use anything you have to hand to defend yourself – keys, an
  umbrella, the heel of your shoe, hairspray.

- Remember that anything you do or any weapon you use is to provide you with an opportunity to get away. Unless you are trained in self-defence, it is absolutely senseless to stay around.
- If you are faced with a knife or another weapon, probably your best defence is to remain calm and try to talk your way out. Whatever you do, it must be your decision.

Physical responses to practise

- If someone grabs your arms with her hands, jerk your arm away in the direction of her thumbs – this is the weakest part of anyone's grip.
- If someone grabs you from behind, bend forward and come back quickly, slamming your head against his face or chin (the back of your head is very hard, but it may hurt you as well).
- If there is a weapon and you think you have a chance to do something to get away, scrape your heel down the inside of her lower leg, or kick her in the knee HARD. Then stamp on her instep with all your weight. Then run!
- Kicking someone in the genitals or poking them in the eyes is not as easy as you might have heard. If you kick up at an attacker, he may just grab your leg and you will end up on the ground. If you try to poke someone in the eye, remember that the juices from the eye will get under your fingernail and be very squishy! If I hear you saying 'yuck', do not try it. Only ever try something you can carry through or you might just do enough to make the attacker even more angry.
- The best advice is to practise the two or three techniques you think you could use until they are automatic.

- Finally, if you are attacked, tell someone – ring the police, talk to a parent, a teacher, a friend. Do not keep it to yourself.

Chapter 14 Addiction

Purpose: To introduce the issue of addiction
Time: 30–45 minutes
Materials: Chalkboard or flipchart, paper

The purpose of this lesson (or lessons) is to provide an introduction from which to study particular areas, such as drug abuse problems, in more depth and in the context of addiction.

   You can start by asking the students the following questions.

What is addiction?

Write the definitions from the students on the board and discuss them. If you need a definition to work with, use:

   Addiction is compulsive behaviour or activity which the addict cannot control or give up. The addiction meets some perceived need of the addict.

What are some forms of addiction?

Have the students break into small groups for five minutes and brainstorm. Compile their ideas on the board.

   If you need to supplement their ideas, suggest:

Alcohol	Gambling
Cigarettes	Sex
Cannabis	Cleanliness (Obsessive)
Crack	Eating
Cocaine	Shopping
Solvents	Lying
Heroin	Stealing/Shoplifting
Marijuana	Bullying
Aspirin	Work

Why do some people become addicts?

Again, ask the students to do group work, but allow enough time for them to come up with at least five reasons.

The addict may be feeling some of the following:

Insecure	Guilty
Vulnerable	Humiliated
Lonely	Picked on
Unhappy	Distrustful
Unloved	Powerless
Rejected	Self-hatred
Ashamed	Depressed
Confused	Curious

Although people who become addicts are usually desperately looking for a way to feel good, it is possible that the addiction started because they were curious about 'trying' something such as drugs that were offered to them. To continue with the addictive habit, however, indicates a basic problem such as those we have listed.

Have the students brainstorm what people think they get out of the addictive habit, whatever that habit may be.

Suggestions

Comfort
Identity
Self-confidence
Support
Power
Love

What do YOU *think addicts get from their addiction?*

Suggestions

More problems
Become dependent
Lose more control
Depression
Eating disorders
Strange behaviours
Dangerous behaviours

What do people need in order not to become addicts?

Suggestions

Love
Security
To know that it is all right to be vulnerable
Guidelines

Friends
To feel happy or satisfied
To feel a sense of accomplishment

If students can begin to understand the reasons for addictive behaviour, it will help them to put the problem of drug use into context.

Follow-up

To follow up on this idea, ask the students to prioritise how they feel about the various forms of addiction, that they listed. Put the words such as work, cannabis, cleanliness, cigarettes on separate pieces of paper. Working in groups, agree as a group on which addictions are the 'worst' and which are the 'best'. This should provoke discussion about how people deal with addictive behaviours and how those behaviours affect the people around them.

When the students have prioritised, have each group report back to the class. Discuss the differences in the priorities listed by the groups.

If someone you lived with was addicted, which of these addictions would affect you the most? The least? Why?

'How can people who are addicted be helped'.

Without the underlying problems being sorted out, people who are addicted will substitute one addiction for another. For example, giving up cigarettes may lead to over-eating of boiled sweets; giving up the liquid drug of alcohol may lead to taking on another comforter such as incessant exercise. One question here is: what are 'acceptable' addictive behaviours – something the students will have discussed when prioritising.

In order to help the students answer the question about helping addicts, you may want to encourage the students to investigate the various forms of addiction and have local experts come in to talk.

Ask the students to choose which areas of addiction they would like to find out more about and ask them to report to the class. Sources of further information are included in the 'Where to get help' section at the end of this manual. More information is available from the Teachers Advisory Council on Alcohol and Drug Education (TACADE).

Chapter 15 Gambling

Purpose: To begin to understand the problem of gambling
Time: 30–45 minutes
Materials: Paper, chalkboard or flipchart

One way to begin the lesson is to ask the students the following questions:

- What is gambling?
- Why do you think that it can be a problem for young people?
- Without mentioning names, could anyone here talk about someone they know who might have had a gambling problem, such as being addicted to arcade machines?

If the students are having difficulty with the concept of gambling, perhaps the following story will help stimulate discussion.

> David started playing fruit machines just for fun at the age of 11. At first he played in his spare time, after school and at the weekends. By the time he was 12, he began to miss the odd day of school to go to the arcades. Now he is 15 and he spends most of his time compulsively playing machines. He has lost 2 stone in weight, his eyes are bloodshot and he has stolen over £10,000 to pay for his habit. He is also aggressive and withdrawn.
>   This is a true story, but the name of the boy has been changed. If you were David's parent, what signs would you think might have warned you that David had a gambling problem?

Have the students talk in small groups and ask them to come up with a list of three or four possible signs or symptoms that might alert them to the problem. When they have finished, bring them together and write their suggestions on the board. They might include:

- Money disappearing
- Possessions disappearing or being sold
- Borrowing money
- Bloodshot eyes
- Lying
- Missing school
- Withdrawn
- Aggressive

Ask the students what they would do if their child were exhibiting these signs.

- What would you do if you knew that your little brother was gambling and stealing money to do it?
- What would you do if your best friend was addicted to using fruit machines?
- What are the laws regarding fruit machines and video arcades?

Have a group of students investigate the current legislation. Some possible sources of information are listed in the 'Where to get help' section of this manual.

Have the students take all the information they acquire and:

- suggest changes in the laws which might protect young people;
- design posters which give other students information which might be helpful;
- invite a speaker from one of the organisations that deal with gambling (see Lesson 11, 'Getting help');
- do a school survey about gambling and publish the results.

Students may also be affected by the gambling of a parent, so it is important to make sure that they are aware of the help organisations.

Where to get help

The following agencies and organisations can listen and give you advice about a variety of problems and concerns. Of course, you can always contact the police, social services and your GP. Someone in your religious community may also be able to help. When contacting any of the listed organisations, you will need to use your own judgement about the suitability of their service or advice for your particular needs.

Abduction (Parental)

The Child Abduction Unit
The Lord Chancellor's Department
81 Chancery Lane
London WC2A 1DD
Tel: 0171 911 7045/7047/7094
If a child has been abducted from the UK, The Child Abduction Unit will give advice about what action you can take and what the British Government can or cannot do to help.

Reunite
National Council for Abducted Children
PO Box 4
London WC1X 8XY
Tel: 0171 404 8356
A booklet entitled *Child abduction* is available from Reunite.

Abuse

Child Abuse Prevention
The Lodge
Cherry Orchard Hospital
Dublin 10.
Tel: 00 3531 6232358/6233893
Provides training for the prevention of child abuse.

Child protection societies
Provide help and advice or referral information about protecting children from child abuse:

Irish Society for the Prevention of Cruelty to Children (ISPCC)
20 Molesworth Street
Dublin 2
Tel: 010 3531 6794944

National Society for the Prevention of Cruelty to Children (NSPCC)
Freephone 0800 800500 24-hour telephone helpline

Royal Scottish Society for the Prevention of Cruelty to Children (RSSPCC)
Melville House
41 Polworth Terrace
Edinburgh E11 1NV
Tel: 0131 337 8539

ChildLine
Freepost 1111 (no stamp needed)
London EC4 4BB.
Tel: 0800 1111 24-hours
Charge-free telephone counselling and advice service for children in trouble or danger.

Family Contact Line
30 Church Street
Altrincham
Cheshire WA14 4DW
Tel: 0161 941 4011/4012
Provides a telephone listening service to families. Also has nursery facilities for parents who wish to attend with their children.

Kidscape
152 Buckingham Palace Road
London SW1W 9TR
Send a large stamped addressed envelope for a free copy of *Why my child?*, a 28-page booklet for helping parents cope with the sexual abuse of their child or children. Also available: *Keep them safe*, a 16-page booklet with suggestions for teaching 5- to 11-year-olds ways to stay safe.

AIDS

Your GP or paediatrician should be able to give you advice and can arrange for testing, if necessary.

For free leaflets and booklets, contact your local health education unit, which is listed in the telephone directory under the name of your Health Authority.

To obtain a copy of *AIDS: what everyone needs to know*, write to:

Dept A
PO Box 100
Milton Keynes MK1 1TX.

To obtain a copy of the British Medical Association's 70 page guide entitled *AIDS and you* send £1.95 to:

British Medical Association
Tavistock Square
London WC1H 9JP.

You can also contact:

Health Information Service
Tel: 0800 665544

Health Literature Line
Tel: 0800 555777

These lines are run by the Department of Health.

Health Call:
0898 600 699 gives recorded general information on AIDS.
0898 600 900 gives recorded specific information on AIDS.

National Aids Helpline
PO Box 1577
London NW1 3DW
Helpline 0800 5687123. 24-hours.
All calls are free and confidential and you can call at any time to talk to a trained counsellor.

Terrence Higgins Trust
52–54 Grays Inn Road
London WC1X 8JU
Tel: 0171 831 0330. 10.00 a.m. to 5.00 p.m. Monday–Friday
Helpline: 0171 242 1010. 3.00 p.m. to 10.00 p.m. every day.
Legal Line: 071 405 2381. 7.00 p.m. to 9.00 p.m. Wednesday
Offers help and counselling to people with HIV or AIDS.

Positively Women
5 Sebastian Street
London EC1V 0HE
Helpline: 0171 490 2327 noon to 2.00 p.m. Monday–Friday
Provides a range of free and strictly confidential support services to women with HIV or AIDS. Activities for women and children, and a children's social worker.

Alcohol abuse

For help with dealing with alcohol abuse contact:

Alcoholics Anonymous
Stonebow House
Stonebow
York YO1 2NJ
Tel: 01904 644026

Helplines:

England	0171 352 3001	10.00 a.m. to 10.00 p.m. every day
Scotland	0141 221 9027	24 hours
Wales	01646 695555	24 hours
N. Ireland	01232 681084	9.00 a.m. to 5.00 p.m. Monday–Friday

Al-Anon/Al-Teen
61 Dover Street
London SE1 4YF
Tel: 0171 403 0888
For family, friends and children who have a relative affected by drinking problems.

Alcohol Counselling Service (ACS)
34 Electric Lane
London SW9 8JJ
Tel: 0171 737 3579/3570

Drinkline
13–14 West Smithfield
London EC1A 9DH
Tel: 0171 332 0150
Helpline: 0171 332 0202
Drinkline provides information and advice to callers worried about their own drinking, gives support to the family and friends of people who are drinking and advises callers on where to go for help.

Anorexia/bulimia/other eating disorders

The following organisations will give advice and/or therapy for people suffering from eating disorders.

Birmingham Women's Therapy Centre
43 Ladywood
Middleway
Birmingham B16 8HA
Tel: 0121 455 8677

Eating Disorders Association (EDA)
Sackville Place
44/48 Magdalen Street
Norwich NR3 1JU
Tel: 01603 621414

The National Centre for Eating Disorders
11 Esher Place Avenue
Esher
Surrey KT10 8PU
Tel: 01372 469493

The Promis Recovery Centre
Old Court House
Pinners Hill
Nonington
Dover
Kent CT15 4LL
Tel: 01304 841700

Women's Counselling & Therapy Service
Oxford Chambers
Oxford Place
Leeds LS1 3AX
Tel: 01532 455725

Bereavement

The Compassionate Friends
53 North Street
Bristol BS3 1EN
Tel: 0117 9665202
Helpline: 0117 9539639 9.30 a.m. to 5.00 p.m. Monday to Friday
A nationwide (and international) self help organisation of parents whose child of any age, including adult, has died through accident, illness, murder or suicide. A postal library and leaflets are also available.

Cruse
126 Sheen Road
Richmond
Surrey TW9 1UR
Helpline: 0181 332 7227 9.30 a.m. to 5.00 p.m. Monday-Friday
Offers counselling for all bereavements.

Bullying

ChildLine
0800 1111. 24 hours
Freephone for children to discuss problems, including bullying.

Kidscape
152 Buckingham Palace Road
London SW1W 9TR
Tel: (0171) 730 3300
Send a large stamped addressed envelope for a free 20-page booklet entitled *Stop bullying!* and other information about schools programmes.

Telephone counselling for families available on Tuesdays and Wednesdays from 9.30 a.m. to 4.40 p.m.

Contraception

The following give advice on contraception, pregnancy, or abortion.

The British Pregnancy Advisory Service
7 Belgrave Road
London SW1V 1QB
Tel: 0171 828 2484

Brook Advisory Centre (for young people)
Head Office
153A East Street
London SE17 2SD
Tel: 0171 708 1234

Family Planning Association
27 Mortimer Street
London W1N 7RJ
Tel: 0171 636 7866

Counselling

These organisations offer counselling on family and other problems.

British Association of Counselling (BAC)
1 Regent Place
Rugby
Warwickshire CV21 2VT
Send A5-size stamped addressed envelope for list of local counsellors. Some are free.

Rape Crisis Centre
Tel: London 0171 837 1600
See telephone directory for local numbers.

Samaritans
See telephone directory for local numbers.
Samaritans are trained volunteers who talk with people about problems of depression and suicide.

Women's Therapy Centre
6 Manor Gardens
London N7 6LA
Helpline: 071 263 6200 10.00 a.m. to 4.00 p.m. Monday and Friday 2.00 p.m. to 4.30 p.m.Tuesday, Wednesday and Thursday
Send large stamped addressed envelope for list of groups and activities.

Youth Access (formerly NAYPCAS)
Magazine Business Centre
11 Newarke Street
Leicester LE1 5SS
Tel: 0116 2558763
Provide names and addresses of local free counselling services to young people. Telephone, or write enclosing an stamped addressed envelope.

Drugs

Doctors, social services, police and Citizens Advice Bureaux should be able to advise about drug centres, dial 100 and ask for FREEPHONE 'Drug problems'.
  Leaflets about drugs are available from

The Department of Health
Information Division
Publicity Section
5th Floor Skipton House
80 London Road
Elephant and Castle
London SE1 6LW
or telephone on the Health Literature Line on: 0800 555 777

The Department for Education produces a booklet entitled *Drug abuse and the young, a guide for education service*. It can be obtained by ringing: 0181 533 2000

The Welsh Office produces leaflets and booklets:

Welsh Office
Information Division
Cathays Park
Cardiff CF1 3NQ.

To obtain a leaflet on solvent abuse, *What to do about glue sniffing*, write to:

Solvent Abuse
Dept M50
13–39 Standard Road
London NW10

Adfam National
Chapel House
18 Hatton Place
London EC1N 8ND
Helpline: 0171 405 3923 10.00 a.m. to 5.00 p.m. Monday–Friday
National helpline for the families and friends of drug users, confidential support and information.

Families Anonymous
Unit 37
Doddington & Rollo Community Assoc
Charlotte Despart Avenue
London SW11 5JE
Tel: 0171 498 4680
Families Anonymous self-help groups are for those affected by drug abuse or the related problems of a relative or friend. It is completely independent and allows callers to remain anonymous.

Release
388 Old Street
London EC1V 9LT
Helplines: 0171 729 9904. 10.00 a.m. to 6.00 p.m. Monday–Friday
          0171 603 8654. 24 hours.
A national drugs and legal advice service, which provides a 24-hour helpline for drug users, families and friends.

Society for the Prevention of Solvent Abuse (RESOLV)
St Mary's Chambers
19 Station Road
Stone
Staffordshire ST15 8JP
Tel: 01785 817885/46097
Produces teaching programmes to help encourage young people to resist experimentation. Has videos and books available. For a full list of resources send a large stamped addressed envelope.

Standing Conference on Drug Abuse (SCODA)
Kingsbury House
1–4 Hatton Place
Hatton Garden
London EC1N 8ND
Tel: 0171 430 2341
Will supply a list of local services available throughout the country.

Teachers Advisory Council on Alcohol and Drug Education (TACADE)
1 Hulme Place
The Crescent
Greater Manchester M5 4QA
Provides education and training materials for the formal education system. Write for full list of materials.

Families

Exploring Parenthood (EP)
Latimer Education Centre
194 Freston Road
London W10 6TT
Tel: 0181 960 1678
Provides professional support and advice to all parents who experience problems from time to time. Easy access to professional advice and support.

Family Rights Group
(England and Wales)
The Print House
18, Ashwin Street
London E8 3DL
Advice/Helpline 0171 249 0008 1.30 p.m. to 3.30 p.m. Monday to Friday
Promotes partnership between families and childcare agencies in England and Wales. They offer confidential advice on the telephone or by letter.

Parents Anonymous
6 Manor Gardens
London N7 6LA
Tel: 0171 263 8918. Answerphone – gives telephone numbers of volunteers who are on duty. They aim to give a 24-hour service.
   Offers a listening service plus help and support to parents who are experiencing problems with any issues regarding children and young people.

Parent-Line
Westbury House
57 Hart Road
Thundersley
Essex SS7 3PP
Helpline: 01268 757077. 9.00 a.m. to 6.00 p.m. Monday to Friday
10.00 a.m. to 2.00 p.m. Saturday
After hours number supplied on answerphone.
   Provides support for parents under stress, therefore maximising a family's capacity for its children.

Parent Network
44–46 Caversham Road
London NW5 2DS
Tel: 0171 485 8535
Programmes to equip parents to feel supported and encouraged while doing the most important job of raising children.

Gambling

Gamblers Anonymous and Gam-Anon
PO Box 88
London SW10 0EU
Helpline: 0171 384 3040. 24 hours
Gamblers Anonymous is a self help group of men and women who have joined together to do something about their gambling problems. Gam-Anon offers friendship, practical help, comfort and under-standing to families of compulsive gamblers.

UK Forum on Young People & Gambling
11 St. Bride Street
London EC4 4AS
Tel: 01243 538635; contact name: Paul Bellringer
Offers advice to parents and young people with gambling problems. Also offers advice to young people addicted to video games.

Legal advice

The Children's Legal Centre
20 Compton Terrace
London N1 2UN
Helpline: 0171 359 6251. 2.00 p.m. to 5.00 p.m. Monday to Friday
Gives advice about law and policy affecting children and young people in England and Wales.

Citizens Advice Bureau
See telephone directory for local numbers.
   Will give details of services available and advice on how to get help

Self-defence

Contact your local council or the library for information about self defence classes in your area.

The Suzy Lamplugh Trust
14 East Sheen Avenue
London SW14 8AS
Tel: 0181 392 1839
The Trust has produced material such as videos and leaflets about keeping safe and self-defence particularly aimed at those who work with the public and who may find themselves in a dangerous situation.

Suicide

ChildLine
Tel: 0800 1111   24 hours.
ChildLine has a FREEPHONE service for children to discuss any problem

Kidscape
152 Buckingham Palace Road
London SW1W 9TR
For a copy of the free leaflet entitled *Suicide and young people* send a large stamped addressed envelope.

Samaritans
See telephone directory for local number.
24-hour helplines to listen to any problems, including feeling suicidal

Telephone services

Message Lines and Premium Calls

Helplines:
   0800 500 212 to register complaints about any telephone service lines run by BT.
   0800 800 810 to arrange to block telephone service line numbers so that they cannot be dialed from your telephone.
   Nuisance callers: a leaflet giving guidance on how to deal with abusive or nuisance telephone calls and what BT can do to help. Available free from BT Customer Service.

ictim support

Victim Support Scheme
National Office
Cranmer House
39 Brixton Road
London SW9 6DZ
Tel: 0171 735 9166
A nationwide network of support groups offering practical help and advice to victims of violence and crime. You can find the number of your local branch either by contacting the office listed above or by looking in your local directory.

Books and Training Materials

Books for young teens/children

Boy
Roald Dahl
Penguin

Into his description of a charmed childhood spent in Wales and
Norway, the author weaves the story of the cruel and barbaric treatment he received at an English public school.

The Bullies meet the Willow Street kids
Michele Elliott
Pan MacMillan

In this sequel to *The Willow Street Kids* (see below), it is not only
Marilyn who finds herself the victim of bullying at the new school.
Gill, Charlie and the rest also encounter Liz and her gang, both in and
out of school.

The Willow Street kids
Michele Elliott
Pan MacMillan

Based on true stories of children's experiences and written in an
entertaining way, this book will help children figure out what to do in
a variety of situations – bullying, getting lost, stranger danger and
unwelcome advances from known adults. Chosen for the 'Good Book
Guide'.

Books for teens

Bullies
Ed Wicke
Kingsway

Alex was the world's greatest expert on bullies. One night, after
dealing with the bullies, Alex had a dream – in the end the bullies
didn't stand a chance.

Bully
Yvonne Coppard
Bodley Head Children's Books

Kerry knew it would happen again – the bullies would be waiting at the gate. Alone and friendless, Kerry is a prime target for the bullies. But Kerry eventually triumphs.

Don't pick on me: how to handle bullying
Rosemary Stones
Piccadilly Press

This book discusses why people bully and what you can do to change things. It incorporates several of the Kidscape suggestions to stop bullying.

Out in the open: a guide for young people who have been sexually abused
Ouaine Bain and Maureen Sanders
Virago

A useful book for young people to help them come to terms with having been abused.

Too close encounters and what to do about them
Rosemary Stones
Methuen

Based on common sense and practical strategies for dealing with everything from flashers to rape, this guide is full of valuable ideas for young people.

Books for adults

Anorexia nervosa: a guide for sufferers and their families
R.L. Palmer
Penguin

Discusses the causes, symptoms and treatment of anorexia in light of current medical opinion. The author gives practical suggestions for dealing with the problem.

Bullies and their victims in schools
Valerie Besag
Open University

Valuable research into relationships, bullies, victims, families and the social behaviour of children, with practical strategies for dealing with bullying.

Bullying, a practical guide to coping for schools
Michele Elliott (ed.)
Longman

Provides practical ideas for teachers and other school personnel to use in dealing with bullying. It explores ways to help bullies and victims, strategies for schools, and suggestions for playgrounds and how to set up 'bully courts'.

Bullying at school: what we know and what we can do
Dan Olweus
Blackwell

This book from the recognised international expert in the field of bullying gives effective ways of counteracting and preventing bullying. The facts about bullying, its causes and consequences are clearly presented.

Caring for the suicidal
John Eldrid
Constable

From the director of the Central London branch of the Samaritans, this book is based on years of experience and is full of practical, down-to earth advice.

Child abuse: The developing child
Ruth S. Kempe and C. Henry Kempe
Fontana

Clearly written comprehensive guide to understanding child abuse.

The common secret: sexual abuse of children
Ruth S. Kempe and C. Henry Kempe
Freeman

From the respected pioneers in the field of child abuse, this book examines child sexual abuse in all its forms, from paedophilia to child pornography to incest.

Cry hard and swim
Jacqueline Spring
Virago

In letters to her mother, poems and narrative, the painful story of father–daughter incest emerges. Through therapy and hard work Jacqueline heals herself and helps others.

Drug warning
David Stockley
Optima

An illustrated guide for parents and teachers which will give you information on treatment and where to get help.

Female sexual abuse of children: the ultimate taboo
Michele Elliott (ed)
Longman

In this pioneering study, the testimony of survivors and of professionals who have worked with them and with abusers bears witness to sexual abuse of children by women.

Fighting, teasing and bullying
Dr John Pearce
Thorsons

If your child is a victim of bullying or a bully, this book will help you to recognise the problems and offer useful strategies to help children learn self-confidence.

For your own good: The roots of violence in child rearing
Alice Miller
Virago

Explores attitudes that emphasise discipline and obedience and the links to such authoritarians as Hitler, who was abused as a child.

Helping children cope with stress
Ursula Markham
Sheldon Press

Helps you to recognise the symptoms of stress and offers advice for particular problems and for generally equipping children to deal with stressful situations.

How to stand up for yourself
Dr Paul Hauck
Sheldon Press

How to feel good about yourself and get your own way without taking advantage of other people is the basis of this very useful little book.

Keeping safe, a practical guide to talking with children
Michele Elliott
Hodder/Headline Coronet Books

Easily understood, step-by-step guide to talking with teenagers and children about keeping safe from a variety of dangers includin bullying, sexual abuse, drugs, AIDS, video nasties, gambling, trave ling by public transport.

Practical approaches to bullying
Peter Smith (ed.)
David Fulton

Collection of reading covering classroom based intervention and th use of drama to deal with bullying.

Substance dependency: a professional guide
Andrew Shephard
Venture Press

A guide to new approaches to dealing with dependency on drug solvent and alcohol. The author explores ways to overcome depen dency and reasons why people become addicted.

Victims no longer
Mike Lew
Cedar Books/Heinemann

An essential book for men and boys who are survivors of sexual abuse It breaks down one of the final barriers and helps men to come to term with their feelings.

Training package for front-line carers

Protecting children: training pack for front-line carers
Michele Elliott
HMSO

Sponsored by the Department of Health, this package consists of a manual and video to help front-line carers such as foster parents teacher, health visitors and others to understand the problem of chilc abuse and to have practical ways to help children who have beer abused. Available from Kidscape and HMSO.

Kidscape child protection programmes for schools

Kidscape child protection programme (ages 5–11)
Michele Elliott
Kidscape

Comprehensive personal safety programme which deals with gettin lost, bullying, stranger danger, potential abuse from known adults

Includes an illustrative video for adults, lessons, exercises and follow-up activities for children, posters, leaflets and ideas for adapting and using the materials with children of different abilities and with special educational needs.

Kidscape under-fives manual
Michele Elliott
Kidscape

Provides lessons for young children and for children for whom English is a second language. It is also appropriate for children with special educational needs.

Talking books for the blind

Preventing child sexual assault
Michele Elliott

Practical advice about talking with children. Available from Royal National Institute for the Blind Library: catalogue no. T5548/2 cassettes. Tel: 0345 023153

Videos

There has been a recent flood of 'prevention' videos into the UK, the vast majority of which have come from Canada and the USA. The videos are intended to make children confident to deal with the possibility that someone might try to touch them in an inappropriate way.
There are several problems with this approach:

- Teenagers should be introduced to the ideas of keeping safe in an inteactive relationship with a responsible adult.
- Videos do not provide sufficient flexibility to deal sensitively with this subject with groups of teenagers
- Most of the videos do not give enough emphasise to good hugs and kisses and positive relationships with adults. Young people could get the message that 'it is best not to trust people'.
- Many videos deal only with sexual abuse, instead of putting the problem into the context of the wider safety message.
- Adults may think that teenagers understand what to do because they have seen the video, and they may therefore be left more vulnerable because they have not understood.
- Some of the videos are too long, too gimmicky and too confusing.

There is no substitute for discussion with young people, particularly in an area as important as keeping them safe. When teenagers, parents and teachers have been through a comprehensive programme and are familiar with all the issues, some videos might prove useful as part of a follow-up lesson. The adult showing the video will then know how to deal with questions; parents will have had meetings and many will have already approached the subject with their teenagers because of the lessons and the material sent home. Once this process has been set up, a video could be used as a tool, but not as the primary means, to help keep children safe.

However, there is a video on bullying which many schools have found useful. *Sticks and stones* (Central Television, Birmingham). Made in consultation with Kidscape, *Sticks and stones* deals with secondary students and the problem of bullying. It includes a mock 'bully court', a bully in prison talking about his days as a bully, and dramatisations of a boy and a girl being bullied by a gangs of kids. It can be shown to upper junior and secondary students. Running time 20 minutes; cost £25.85 (including P & P and VAT) from Kidscape. (Note: the price may change – it is listed here as a guide).